LIND

DAUGHTER
of the KING

Finding Our True Identity in Christ

UNITED HOUSE

Unless otherwise indicated, all Scripture quotations are taken from
The Holy Bible, English Standard Version® (ESV®) Copyright © 2001 by Crossway, a publishing ministry of Good News Publishers. All rights reserved.

ESV Text Edition: 2016
The Holy Bible, English Standard Version (ESV) is adapted from the Revised Standard Version of the Bible, copyright Division of Christian Education of the National Council of the Churches of Christ in the U.S.A. All rights reserved.

Scripture quotations marked TPT are from The Passion Translation®. Copyright © 2017, 2018 by Passion & Fire Ministries, Inc. Used by permission. All rights reserved. ThePassionTranslation.com.

Scripture quotations marked (NLT) are taken from the Holy Bible, New Living Translation, copyright ©1996, 2004, 2015 by Tyndale House Foundation. Used by permission of Tyndale House Publishers, Carol Stream, Illinois 60188. All rights reserved.

ISBN: 978-1-952840-20-3

UNITED HOUSE Publishing
Waterford, Michigan
info@unitedhousepublishing.com
www.unitedhousepublishing.com

Interior design:
Matt Russell, Marketing Image, mrussell@marketing-image.com

Printed in the United States of America
2022—First Edition

SPECIAL SALES
Most UNITED HOUSE books are available at special quantity discounts when purchased in bulk by corporations, organizations, and special-interest groups. For information, please e-mail orders@unitedhousepublishing.com

This book is dedicated to my amazing husband Jason to whom I'm forever grateful for your support along this adventure.

To my boys: Toby, Wyatt, and Titus, remember who you are - sons of the King, mighty warriors for His Kingdom, don't let anyone tell you otherwise.

To my daughter, who I have yet to meet, may you grow up to be a strong and wise daughter of Zion.

Foreword

There are many things I can say about the author of this book. I remember when I met Lindsey. I had seen her a few times at church, but truly did not know who she was. She was the lady who sat two rows from the front and who worshiped like no one else was around. The one encounter we had in the parking lot with a follow-up phone call left me certain that this was a woman who truly loved the Lord, but more importantly, she was a woman who wanted everyone else to know about her Abba. She unreservedly shared her story and her journey with me. What struck me the most was how aligned we were in our passion for women, a burning desire to see them set free, delivered from the lies of the enemy, and walking in the knowledge of the power they carry within them. This shared passion led us and our dear friend, Chiderah to start the podcast, Arrow Women.

Lindsey is a spitball of fire, a prayer warrior, an intercessor, and generally a gift to the body of Christ. She is a mother of three young boys and a wife to her Jas. She pours out herself to her three boys and her husband, sensitive to the move of the Lord in their lives, as she puts her family first knowing that it is her first ministry. As if raising young warriors was not enough, she mentors, leads, and encourages women in our church, and has now written this book to help women find their true identity in God. By the way, this is her second book. Her first book is titled *45 Days of Prayer*.

Many of us have struggled with insecurity, rejection, guilt, brokenness, and a low self-esteem, battling internally with understanding who we are, weighing the relevance of the world's opinions and standards, failing to recognize that who we are is fundamentally rooted in who God is and in our understanding of how He sees us. We define and redefine who we think we are over the course of time, as often as we can, based on where we find ourselves and based on external circumstances such as, media, cultural expectations, relationships, and our environment.

In this book, Lindsey walks us through the process of understanding our identity as daughters of Christ by first acknowledging who God is and then revealing what is written in the Scriptures about us. In order to free ourselves from the lies and fully embrace who we are in Christ, we must choose to surrender and then begin to walk by faith, living out our identity grounded on truth and in relationship with God. When we take those steps, we no longer seek validation and acceptance from others. We understand that our past, our current situation, people's perception of us and our external circumstances are not a reflection of who we are, and our worth is not in them. We recognize that we are chosen, holy, blameless, loved, called, blessed, masterpieces carefully crafted for a purpose. We approach life with boldness and courage, capable because of the power of God at work in us.

Are you lost, discouraged, unsure, weak, constantly sizing

yourself up against others, broken, ashamed? Then this book is for you. I invite you to open up these pages and let Lindsey speak to you from her heart, from Abba's heart. Even if you were certain about your identity, I still invite you to let her words refresh your spirit. You will find encouragement and breakthrough, clarity and perspective, freedom and power, and most importantly, you'll discover that you are who God says you are and because He is truth and what He says is the truth, you are the daughter of a king.

Ogechi Umeh
co-founder of Arrow Women podcast

Contents

Introduction

Who am I?

As you read this question, what's the first word or phrase that comes to mind? Grab a sticky note and a pen, and write it down.

The goal of this book is to shed light on who we really are, so I want us to write out where we're starting from as we embark on this journey. With your answer in mind, I want to ask you another question: What does it mean to be a daughter or a son of God? We often hear these words and even claim we are God's children but do we really understand what that means?

See, I believe we are children of God and remain so even amid an identity crisis. I'm not talking about our culture; I'm talking about our churches. So many who claim to be children of God talk about sonship and daughtership as one of their roles in life, as though it were an accessory to who they are rather than it literally being their whole identity.

Trust me—I was one of them. I knew I was a believer and a daughter of the King because I had placed my faith in Jesus and called upon His name. But, had you asked me anything else, I couldn't tell you much about my inheritance, my authority, or the true heart of the Father. I thought those who claimed to hear the voice of God were a little crazy. Coming from a medical background, as a nurse, I viewed life according to the natural, physical realm—what my five senses could perceive. I didn't have a category for living according to the spirit, as though the spiritual realm was a genuine reality. Even when it came to spiritual warfare, yes, I had some head knowledge, but I never truly understood it. I grew up hearing people recite Ephesians 6 saying my battle was not against flesh and blood, yet I found this confusing because what I was seeing through my natural "flesh and blood" eyes was that a person was being rude, greedy, or difficult in a conflict. I didn't understand the spiritual activity behind the conflict with the person.

With the root cornerstone being Jesus Christ crucified, we are going to begin to dig into our true identity as sons and daughters of God and how this is a core foundation for our entire lives; one we cannot ignore. From the way we see each member of the Trinity, to our understanding and perception of things in both the natural and the spiritual realms, we will dive into what it looks like to walk everyday life in the truth of who we really are as children of God.

My prayer is by the end of this book, all of our answers to the question "Who am I?" will align with the perspective of our heavenly Father, that we will know without a shadow of a doubt who we are in Him, and that we will be compelled by the massive implications for our lives both here on earth and for all of eternity. We have the privilege of walking in relationship with the Father, hearing His heart, being led by His Spirit, and operating in the authority He has given us. We are His image-bearers, created for a purpose. That is what I want you to see and hear in the pages of this book: you were created for a purpose, and there is so much more for you than you may think or know.

One

My Encounter with Jesus

*And they have conquered him by the blood of the
Lamb and by the word of their testimony, for
they loved not their lives even unto death.*

Revelation 12:11

Looking back as I write this, I have been encouraged to see
how far the Lord has brought me. He has taught me so much
about who He is, who I am because of His Son, and the
spiritual authority I have because of His victory at the cross
through Jesus' death and resurrection. Jesus conquered so
much in those three days between His death and resurrection.
He established our salvation and our ability to go to Heaven.
We were given an inheritance. We were set free from the
bondage of sin, death, and the reign of the enemy over us. We
are no longer slaves to the former law, but servants to Christ
and His righteousness. Jesus conquered death, and He set us
free to start walking in communion with the Father. He took
everything upon Himself—every evil thought, word, curse, or
deed—and bore the pain and the wrath of His Father so that we
could be set free from the law once and for all. His own Father
turned away from Him while Jesus was dying on the cross.
Can you fathom that? But it was because of His great love for
His children (Romans 5:8) and Jesus' heart of obedience to His

Father (Philippians 2:8) that we are set free to live in Christ.

I want to spread this message with my testimony as my motivation. My experience is one of fear turned into victory, and I can't help but tell the story of this victory to anyone who will listen. I can no longer just sit on the sidelines and watch as many other Christians walk around thinking the same things I did about our Father. I want them to experience the freedom I have and walk in it daily.

While there's more to my testimony than what you are about to read here, I primarily want to focus on one specific encounter I had with Jesus in the fall of 2018. My husband, Jason, and I felt like we were being called to add a third child to our family. In preparation for this, I made an appointment with my OB/GYN to have my intrauterine device (IUD) removed. Little did I know, this appointment would forever mark me and change the course of my life.

On July 10, 2018, I walked into the doctor's office, excited to start a new adventure of motherhood. However, I left that office terrified of the unknown and anxious about the future. What was supposed to be a routine removal turned into a terrifying ordeal where they were unable to locate the IUD. The doctor ordered an invasive ultrasound procedure in which they would have to numb me, open up my uterus, and go in to look for it. All of this scared me immensely.

I was told by the physician to schedule an ultrasound procedure to remove the IUD, however, he never mentioned ordering medications. I found out he'd ordered medications when my pharmacy called saying that my prescriptions were ready.

Confused, I called the doctor's office, and they directed me to another person who started to explain the procedure my doctor wanted me to schedule and the medications I would need to take before the procedure. I hung up the phone confused, frustrated, scared, and fearful of the invasive procedure described to me. I was also determined not to take many of the ordered medications because I knew what they were, how they would make me feel, and that their after-effects could linger and cause problems if and when we conceived in the months ahead. I remember telling Jason that night that I was unsure about the whole thing and I was uncomfortable with taking some of those medications. He told me that everything would be okay, but I didn't feel any better. That is when I began listening to and speaking lies over myself-lies about the Lord punishing me for sins from my college days before coming back to Him. I thought, "God, haven't I obeyed you? Have I not been good enough? Haven't I already asked for forgiveness for X, Y, and Z?"

These thoughts and questions opened the door for more lies to start filling my mind. I would start to rehearse all the what-if scenarios in my head. *What if the IUD punctured my uterus, I have to have major surgery, and will never bear any more kids? What if the IUD moves somewhere in my body, and they are unable to get it out?* Any medical worst-case scenario that I could think of was what went through my mind; especially after some nursing friends told me horror stories of patients they'd had with IUD issues. I know they meant no harm, but their stories increased my anxiety, and I started to let the lies take root in my spirit.

As I let my mind be consumed by fear, I allowed the enemy

to have a foothold in my evenings, especially as I was starting to fall asleep. My dreams were plagued by fear, and I often woke myself or my husband by screaming for help. I can't even begin to recall the number of times I would wake up terrified and covered in sweat. This went on for several weeks. The darkness scared me. Then, I began seeing and feeling demonic activity. I remember sensing them at the foot of my bed taunting me. "Look at you; you're going crazy. You must be losing your mind. You'd better not tell anyone or they will think you're crazy and admit you to a psych ward." My nights were tormenting.

During the day, I felt lost in my thoughts, often wondering if I was going crazy. I didn't even talk with my husband about what I was experiencing. He would comment that I seemed anxious, but I was afraid to talk about what I was hearing and seeing. The biggest lie I started to believe was that I was crazy and that they would put me in a mental hospital if I told anyone. I didn't tell my friends. I didn't tell my family. I let the questions in my mind win and continue to torment me. I felt like I was sinking into a dark hole and nobody knew. I would put on a smile during the day or when I was around others, but inside my mind, I had so many questions, thoughts, and lies swirling around. There were many times during the day that I would read my Bible and pray, but it felt like nothing was there. The only peace I would find was when I played worship music loudly, and as the lies and fear were drowned out, I would lie on the floor weeping and crying out, "Lord, help me."

In August of 2018, the Lord forever changed me. I was dreaming again, but this dream was different from the nightmares I had been having. In my dream, I was in a park, and although it seemed like it should have been a beautiful day because the sun was out, it was not. The sky above me was black, but I could see sunshine and clear skies everywhere else. I was sitting at a picnic table on a hill by a tree, terrified, aware of dark enemy forces swirling all around, desperate for it all to go away. I felt so overwhelmed and terrified by the sight of the darkness surrounding me, but I couldn't take my eyes off of it. I started to feel depressed and anxious, fearing that the darkness would never go away. I felt insane. That's when I heard my name called.

"Lindsey."

I turned to look, and sitting in front of me was Jesus. His face was so full of love and compassion. I remember the brightness radiating off Him. He reached across the table and grabbed my face in His hands and said: "Lindsey, I want you to keep your eyes on me, not the darkness." It was those words that forever changed me. The look in His eyes was like nothing I had ever seen or felt before. He had been sitting there with me all along. His eyes had so much love, peace, and gentleness in them. I felt no shame or guilt, just an overwhelming wave of peace and His tangible love for me. The light surrounding Him broke the darkness that was surrounding me, and I couldn't take my eyes off of Him. I still get emotional at the thought because that encounter with Jesus marked me forever. It was then that all of the voices started to quiet down. They were there, but I couldn't hear them anymore. Light started radiating not just from Jesus but from the heavens. The enemy tactics were failing. He was still shooting arrows at me, but every one of them fell away. After this encounter, Psalm 23 came into my mind.

The Lord is my shepherd; I shall not want. He makes me lie down in green pastures. He leads me beside the still waters. He restores my soul. He leads me in paths of righteousness for his name's sake. Even though I walk through the valley of the shadow of death, I will fear no evil, for you are with me; your rod and your staff, they comfort me. You prepare a table before me in the presence of my enemies; you anoint my head with oil; my cup overflows. Surely goodness and mercy shall follow me all the days of my life, and I shall dwell in the house of the Lord forever.

Psalm 23

For the first time, I understood. The Lord restores my soul, and He leads me in paths of righteousness for His name's sake. Even though we walk in the valley of the shadow of death, we can walk and fear no evil. He brings comfort in those moments.

He prepares a table in the presence of my enemies. These words jumped off the pages of my Bible. He is always there. We have to have eyes to see His presence. Are our eyes fixed on the trials, suffering, and darkness, or do we have eyes to see Him? I think He wants many of us to open our eyes to see that the table is literally sitting right there for us to join. Right in the midst of the enemy darts flying— sickness, barrenness, fear, anxiety, darkness—whatever we are facing, He has a lavish table sitting there, and all He wants us to do is look at Him and sit down. I found out the table had been right there all along! I don't want anyone else to miss it. I don't want anyone to miss the goodness, the love, and the peace flowing from His eyes and everything that comes from being in His presence.

That one moment with Him changed so much. It touched and marked me. I am not the same person I was before that dream. I can't be silent anymore. I can't let anyone else miss this. That is why I'm writing this book. Just like I said at the beginning of this chapter, it was the encounter with Jesus that changed me. It was one of the first times I truly felt free of the condemnation of my past. With one look, it was like He began to heal my heart. Without saying much, it was as though He was pulling off lies I had believed and began speaking truth into that area. This is where He started to show me who I really am and what is spoken in the Scriptures is real. He is loving, He is kind, He is compassionate, He is full of peace. He leaves the ninety-nine and goes after the one lost sheep. But what most impacted me was that He knew *me*! He said my name. *"Lindsey."* He knew me intimately; He knew who I was individually, apart from everyone else in the world. As I write this, the fact that He knew my name blows my mind still. I mean, think of all the people who have walked the earth, yet Jesus knew me by name.

If you, like me, feel like that lost sheep—unseen, unsure of who you are, aware of the Word of God, but not fully understanding what it means when He calls you daughter or beloved—I want you to know that He loves you, He is with you, and *He knows your name.* He knows everything about you. He knows that you don't feel seen. He knows that you are struggling to understand who you are at your job or in your home, or even who you are in general. I believe that He wants you to know right now, as you read this page, that He is with you, and He is for you. He is with you wherever you might be-in darkness, where nights seem terrifying, in any situation that seems hopeless, amid the suffering and pain that you are enduring that just seems unfair, or even in the mundane as you care for your family. He sees you and knows you! There is nobody else like you, and He made you on purpose.

I know He is doing much for me and will continue to do much in me, but what I want us to see, hear, and read are the things He has been teaching me since that moment. My prayer is that these things will help you start to see God for who He really is and that they stir up something in your spirit, making you want to sit at His feet and just lay your head in His lap.

There has not been one minute that we have been forsaken. We have been set free; we are His beloved, heirs to His throne. I believe it is in God's lap where the journey of our search for true identity begins.

Two

Who is God the Father?

If we are to truly understand our identity in Christ, we need to understand the nature of our Heavenly Father. We need to understand God's nature so that we can better understand what it means to be His children. Understanding His nature helps us recognize when things in our lives don't match up with what He desires, how He would speak, or things He would do. I am by no means saying that I fully understand everything about God, but I have learned much about Him by digging deeper into a relationship with Him, seeking Him, crying out to Him, and learning to listen. This has allowed me to get to know Him as my loving Father. You see, His heart is and has always been for His children. He longs to have an intimate relationship with us and to have us come to Him for everything. The love He has for us is beyond anything we could ever fathom, and it is deeper than any love we have experienced here on Earth. It is wider than the east is from the west, and it is never-ending, no matter how far we run from Him. The truth of who He really is, I believe, is not at all like many of us grew up understanding or believing. If we really knew Him, we would never want to leave His side.

So many of us, including me, have walked away from our faith at some point, not understanding who God really is. I walked away from Him my senior year of high school. I didn't understand why the things I had prayed for didn't come to pass; that brokenness and death came instead. I'd lost some close friends after my boyfriend and I ended our two-year relationship, and around the same time, my "second mom's" cancer came back aggressively. After praying for her to be healed and watching the elders at our church anoint her and pray over her, I believed that the Lord would heal her. She went into remission, and I was expecting her to fully heal.

She'd played a big role as a mentor and leader in my life. She seemed to always show kindness and love to me in every season, and when I was hurt, she would speak encouragement without judgment. I'll never forget the October of my senior year when we were on a church youth retreat, and she took four of us girls out for pizza. I remember piling into her big fifteen-passenger van, laughing and being goofy, and her just listening to us talk about our struggles. That was one of my last memories with her before she passed away just a few months later in January. I struggled with anger towards God as I experienced her death and the loss of my friends and boyfriend.

The things I believed in seemed to be crumbling around me. The people that I'd trusted seemed to turn away and reject me, so I began to turn away from everything I knew and all the labels I felt people had put on me. I was hurting. I struggled with body image, how people saw me, and I took every critical word they spoke about me and tried to fix it myself. On the surface, I did my best to please those around me, but deep inside, I was broken, fearful, and angry. I felt unseen and unheard, even by those closest to me and even by many who called themselves believers. Only seeing my pain, I didn't understand at the time that maybe they too were hurting. Looking back, I see that we were just putting band-aids on our wounds without really getting to the deep reasons behind them. I remember telling God that I couldn't walk with Him anymore because I didn't want to be like the people I saw around me. I remember saying to Him out loud, "I'm gonna go do my own thing until I believe that You are really for me, and if You are for me, then I will follow You and do whatever You call me to do."

You see, I took Him to be what I had heard or seen through the perspectives of others. We all have a flawed view of Him at some point because of our flawed relationships. For instance, it can be hard to see God as our perfectly loving Father if we don't have a loving earthly father, so we'll often subtly and even accidentally change the message of who He is based on our own experiences. I think we can also falsely characterize Him based upon the experiences we have had in the church or with authority figures in our lives. But our God is not human. We bear His image, but He is perfect. He doesn't break promises, lie, or discipline with unrighteous anger. He doesn't spew unkind words, and He isn't a hypocrite.

I have gone from seeing Him as a harsh judge, one who would punish His children every time they disobeyed, to seeing Him as loving and full of compassion and mercy; from a God who doesn't hear our cries for healing and restoration to a Father whose heart has always been for renewal. I began to understand when healing doesn't happen, there's so much more going on we may not see or understand. I have also begun to see Him as the light in the darkness. Even in the brokenness of this world that is so full of hate, death, and evil, I started seeing His light break through the darkness. I like to picture a dark tunnel when you start to see light peeping in; at first, the light seems so small on the other side, but the closer you get to it, the brighter it shines through the darkness.

God is Abba (Father)

We see God's fatherly characteristics in how He provides for us, how He disciplines us, and how He protects us, but what hits me the most is how He longs for an intimate relationship. He longs to just spend time with us. He holds us close and says, "Come and lay your head on my chest." It is then we start to see Him, not through what we read but through what we experience in relationship with Him by calling out and listening, just like a child would cry out for their parents when they needed them.

It was when I began to see myself as a child, through the eyes of a child, that I began to see how God is like a Father. You see, even as adults, we, at times, long to be held and to just snuggle in close to the arms of a parent or a father figure in our lives. In moments of pain, sadness, and confusion, when it feels like the world is crashing down around us, how comforting it would be to curl up in a ball and just be held in the protective arms of the Father; to run up to Him with no explanation needed and bury our heads in His chest and let it all out. This is digging in deep with Him, allowing Him into every facet and area of our lives and hearts, saying, "I need you. Apart from you, Father, I can't do anything." It is praying and crying out, "Make me more like you, so I can better see your heart for those around me, for my kids, my husband, my co-workers, etc." Or, "Abba, I can't carry this heavy load anymore—the emotions I'm feeling, the sorrow I feel deep in my spirit, the gut-wrenching pain—I just can't bear it anymore, so I'm laying it here and asking you to step in and heal that area completely. I want my soul to radiate with You, not me."

In the last few years, this is where I have often found myself, sitting at His feet, laying my head on His chest to cry and scream when things happen that I don't understand or when the weight of something just seems too much to bear. It is in those moments where I feel His presence the most, wrapping His arms around me and stroking my hair, saying, "It will be alright, my daughter. I know this feels like a lot, but you are stronger than you think. I am right here with you." And He just sits there listening to my heart. These are the moments where I have built intimacy with Him, where I have placed everything at His feet, trusting that He will hold my cares and carry my burden, just like He promises in His Word. Matthew 11:28-30 says, "Come to me, all who labor and are heavy laden, and I will give you rest. Take my yoke upon you, and learn from me, for I am gentle and lowly in heart, and you will find rest for your souls. For my yoke is easy, and my burden is light."

As I write this, I think about the Kristene DiMarco song, "I Am No Victim," where she talks about her confidence that His plans for us are good. You see, we don't have to wonder if He has good plans for us or if He will provide for all our needs. His heart is for us to prosper and to succeed at what He has spoken over us since the beginning of time. Those of us with children can see a glimpse into His heart for us through the way we see our kids. We cherish them, we are delighted by them, and we want the very best for them. We want them to succeed, to prosper in what we see within them.

Sometimes, we can be distracted by the earthly things we think we should attain, and that is when we tend to veer away from what the Lord has called us to. It's like a young child or puppy playing in a field when a butterfly flies by. Instead of playing with the ball or frisbee in front of them, they veer off course to follow the butterfly, forgetting what they were originally doing. When we have lost our way, we can approach Him and allow Him to guide us back on the path He has set before us.

This is the way He disciplines—in love. He allows the Holy Spirit to convict us, giving us a nudge in our spirit when things are not right. It isn't to condemn and bring shame, yet, so many of us walk around feeling shamed and condemned by our past. But, that is not His heart's intent. We forget He is the One who sent his Son to free us from this condemnation and slavery to the law. Romans 8:22 reads, "But now that you have been set free from sin and have become slaves of God, the fruit you get leads to sanctification and its end, eternal life." His conviction doesn't lead to condemnation; rather, it leads to sanctification, pointing out the areas where He wants to make us more like Him and bring out the good fruit within us. Like a loving Father, He wants to point us back to the right path and show us the full potential He sees in us, for He knows the things He has planted deep within us and that they need to be nurtured, watered, and pruned.

I like to picture a game of "Pin the Tail on the Donkey" at a child's birthday party: When you are watching the kid who is blindfolded try to walk and find the donkey, you can't help but start to point them in the right direction, cheering them on and saying, "You can do this; it is literally right in front of you!" You encourage them along the way and also warn them when they are way off. See, the Father is our biggest cheerleader, and He also is loving in His discipline! He sees that so often the correct path is right in front of us, and He cheers for us, corrects us, and tries to point us in the right directions by speaking to us through His written word and His spoken word.

This is why a relationship with the Father is so important. We wouldn't trust the person giving us directions if they were blindfolded too, but we would trust the one who sees the whole plan and direction laid out; right? Yet, so many of us listen to the bystander who is blinded, and we don't trust our Heavenly Father who can see the beginning to the end. Hebrews 12:6 in The Passion Translation says this: "For the Lord's training of your life is the evidence of his faithful love. And when he draws you to himself, it proves you are his delightful child."

His guidance, training, and delight in us show us more of how He loves and cares for us as a Father-one who is always present and makes no mistakes. He always has our best interest in His heart. He repeatedly sees the best in us even if we don't see it. He has always been there for us. As Deuteronomy 31:8 tells us: "It is the Lord who goes before you. He will be with you; he will not leave you or forsake you. Do not fear or be dismayed."

This is how I have begun to see Him, as my true Father. He loves me regardless of any circumstances. He cares about me. He just wants to hold me. He wants the best for me. He sees the good in me. He just loves to be with me, and He loves to speak to me. He feels the same way for all His children!

God is Love

*God, everyone sees your goodness, for your
tender love is blended into everything you do.*

Psalm 145:9, TPT

*O God, how extravagant is your cherishing
love! All mankind can find a hiding place
under the shadow of your wings.*

Psalm 36:7, TPT

God is love. Everything we know about love would not exist if not for God's love. I began to see, as I started to read more and ask Him questions, the way I saw love was so skewed. You see, I haven't met anyone who has ever lived up to the level of love God has for me. I have often viewed the way God loves me through the lens of my experiences, taking this and that and putting it into a category of what His love is like. You can see how far that got me. I saw Him as a punisher every time I sinned, one who accused and cast judgment. I was so stuck on confessing all my sins, I didn't even see how much He loved me and that he'd given everything to rescue me. Yes, I knew that He'd died on the cross because He loved me and sent His Son to take my place, but I didn't really, truly understand just how much He loved me even in the midst of my wretchedness.

Paul's words, *"wretched man that I am,"* are where I kept getting stuck. I forgot that Romans 8:1 immediately follows those words with this: "There is therefore now no condemnation for those who are in Christ Jesus. For the law of the Spirit of life has set you free in Christ Jesus from the law of sin and death." This is what Paul meant, and we need to plant this deep into our core. Yes, we were wretched, but now, we are no longer condemned or slaves to the law because of the love of the Father, who sent His Son to die and take our place on that cross. His death gave me freedom; freedom to sit in the heavenly places and freedom to experience the love of the Father. This is not from behind a closed veil, like in the temple, but face to face. I get to run into His arms. I get to cry out to Him as His beloved daughter. I get to experience His love and pursuit of me.

I believe many of us need to understand that we have been truly forgiven to further understand His love. It's hard for us to understand the love someone else has for us when we feel unloveable or unworthy of their love. We have to get past this to move forward into a relationship. Listen: you are loved. God loved us enough to send His Son to die for us. God spoke life into each one of us. He created everything about us. He knew exactly what time in history to place each one of us for us to live out the purpose He put within us. He knew from the beginning of Creation what we were going to look like, our personalities, our temptations and downfalls, our desires, our creativity, our deepest longings, and everything else about us. Mistakes and all, He sees us for who we are and continues to speak life into us. It took me actually seeing all this to be able to see that His love for me was bigger than any of my past sins and regrets.

His love for us is deeper and wider than everything. I still have a hard time wrapping my mind around that sometimes. If you are struggling to see how God loves us like I was, I would highly encourage you to read Brian and Candace Simmons' book, *The Sacred Journey*. They write: "How amazing is it that God takes His maiden and prepares her to be a glorious bride, transforming her by His tender love. It is time for an identity transplant to occur within her heart.[1] What transforms our identity is the tender love of God speaking life into areas that are broken and filling them with His perfect love. Wow. We see this reflected in Hosea 2:14 which states, "Therefore, behold, I will allure her; and bring her into the wilderness and speak tenderly to her." Right before this verse, we see Hosea given words from the Lord of judgment. In verse 13, the Lord says to Hosea, she "went after her lovers and forgot me." Although the Lord was speaking about Israel at the time, I believe those words are still spoken over us today. It is God's love for us that compels Him to chase after us, His children, even when we have turned and gone after our own ways. Just as verse 14 says, He leads His children into the wilderness to speak tenderly to them and to allure them back to Him. This blows my mind. I would never go after someone who doesn't love me or try to allure them and speak tenderly to them; especially if they had been cheating on me. Yet, this is the love of our Heavenly Father, the Lord God, the Great I Am. It is in His nature to pursue His kids, to draw them out in the wilderness for a time and speak tenderly to them.

I believe that, in life, we will walk through many seasons in the wilderness, where the Lord is trying to draw us back to His heart, to our first true love. He pulls us into the quiet, into a season where it just seems hard. Often, in the wilderness one may feel stuck; it feels like there is nothing in sight, and we are desperate for the voice of the Lord. This could look like a trial, pain, or just a season where He is drawing you deeper into intimacy with Him. He wants us to see more of Him and more of His heart, and when we feel like we just can't keep going, He starts to speak life into us. God shows His tenderness for us in those moments and reveals just how much He loves us and how He cares for us. For me, it was the season where I thought I was going crazy that drove me to Him.

I followed Him into the wilderness, where things seemed quiet, and I felt lost and confused. I was being confronted with things I did not fully understand, but He continued to chase after me. He protected and watched over me during the nights in the wilderness that seemed so dark and cold. Then, in the day, He would lead me to the next place to camp, where He would reveal more of Himself, showing me who He truly was, and uncovering deeply rooted lies and weeds that had grown up in the soil of my heart—lies and weeds that needed to be removed before I could move on. It was in this wilderness season where I truly saw that His heart for me was full of love and my perceptions and viewpoints of Him were not accurate pictures of who He really was.

This is the beauty of walking in a relationship with the Father, understanding that our identity is wrapped up in Him. It is pursuing Him that draws us closer to knowing more of His heart and being able to listen to how His heart beats for us. It is what speaks life into who we are.

God is Light

This is the message we have heard from him and proclaim to you, that God is light, and in him is no darkness at all.

1 John 1:5

For it is you who light my lamp;
the Lord my God lightens my darkness.

Psalm 18:28

There is only One who can light up the darkness: His name is Yahweh, the Creator of all things. I know and believe these words. As you read in my testimony, His presence can bring light into the darkest of places. He is Light and light radiates off Him; nothing can be hidden in darkness when His glory enters in. I had always read this in Scripture, but now I have seen this truth with my own eyes, and it has come alive to me like never before. In my encounter with Him at the picnic table, it was like He spoke my name, and His eyes pierced the darkest of places within me and exposed them with His light. Everything not of Him since then has seemed to begin to fall off: the fear I carried from childhood, the way I saw myself through others' eyes, the anxiety, the doubt. It all fell off, and it was like something awoke and began to shine out of me.

It is hard to put into words, but something forever shifted inside of me. Whenever I start to feel anxious, for example, I now know what to do. I take the anxious thoughts and turn them into truth over myself and the situation. "Abba, my heart is anxious about this situation, and I know that anxiety is not from you. You have told me that I do not need to worry or be anxious, for you have provided for my every need, so I lay down these anxious thoughts and give them to you, and I pick up the belt of truth which says 'do not be anxious in anything' but to turn and give you praise and thanks (Philippians 4:6). So, I give you thanks that I am loved, provided for, and that I have been adopted and made right with you." I then usually will turn to worship music or a psalm to encourage my heart and meditate on the truth He revealed at that moment.

So, what is darkness? For me, it was the unending anxiety and fear that consumed me. I couldn't shake it, and it made my heart race. It was there when I went to sleep, when I woke up, and all throughout the day. Some days, I felt scared and sad; other days, I would just be lost in my thoughts which would spiral downward into fears of harm coming to me or to my loved ones.

A friend of mine has struggled with darkness in the form of irrational anger. She describes it as inner rage that doesn't match the circumstances, and when it comes, she feels stuck and unable to break out of it even though she is aware that it is irrational.

Darkness comes in many forms, but as we know from the natural definition, darkness is the absence of light. So if God is light, then spiritual darkness is the absence of God. In other words, darkness is anything not of God. Outer sin is an obvious form of darkness because we can usually see it, and we know it is not of God. Lies from the enemy, twisted truth or accusations and condemnation are other forms of darkness. Then, there are the more blatant attacks from the enemy, which can sometimes be in the form of physical or mental harm, like the attacks Job endured.

Darkness can also be seen where Satan has a stronghold over a particular person, place, culture, or people. I want to quickly define what I mean by stronghold because I feel like many of us hear this term but don't fully understand its meaning. In Hebrew, the word stronghold is "matsuwd," and it means "to be captured, hunted, the net of a hunter, or the top of a peak, a fortress."[2] Oftentimes, we can feel trapped or captured by a repeating cycle of darkness. It feels like every time we think we have gotten out, we find that we have not escaped it. This is a stronghold.

We can also feel darkness in an atmosphere because of the presence of God within us making us more aware that there is spiritual darkness surrounding us. I have often heard people explain it as a feeling within them, when they walk into an environment where God is absent. An example would be a missionary walking into a city or village where the enemy has operated for long periods of time, and there is no presence of Light except within them. I can testify to this myself. I have walked into environments where the atmosphere felt heavy and overwhelming with the presence of darkness; you can feel the absence of God. It can feel like a heaviness or a thick fog, and it often makes you want to run the opposite direction.

When darkness surrounds us, we can tend to either wallow in it or stumble around, attempting to find a way to bring our happiness or contentment into it through things such as TV binging, eating, shopping, or other activities. We try to take our minds off of the depression or anxiety we are experiencing by distracting ourselves from what is bothering us. These things may feel good at the moment, but that feeling is only temporary, like a small window that opens to let light in but then quickly shuts. I have found that every time I have pursued distractions like that in the past, the light would shine for a bit and then go out. It wouldn't stay ablaze, so I was once again left in the dark. Then, I met Him, Yahweh, the creator of everything. He stepped in and lit up the whole room. His light filled the darkness, and the room never went dark again. That is the kind of effect He has. This is not to say I never again experienced fear or anxiety, but whenever this darkness comes, I now know how to welcome the light of my Father into my circumstances. Peace is always the result.

I know many of us have stumbled around in that darkness, hoping that some light would break through and stay. But I want you to know this, God is the Light that stays. He is the Light that can not be put out. When we allow Him to step in, He literally starts to shine into the darkest of places within us. I have learned that what the psalmist says in Psalm 139:11-12 is true: "If I say, 'Surely the darkness shall cover me, and the light about me be night,' even the darkness is not dark to you; the night is bright as the day, for darkness is as light with you." You see, the psalmist knew all too well, both in the natural and in the spiritual, that wherever the Lord God is, darkness will never be darkness because His light cannot be put out. Glory to God, for His Light literally cannot be put out. Where would I be without it?!

The Father longs for us to invite Him in and allow Him to shine His light into our darkness. It is His heart's desire for us to welcome Him in, to seek Him, and to say, "I need you. Apart from you, I can't do anything." It is this invitation that allows His Light to step in and start to nurture and grow that seed that He planted within us at the time we were conceived. It's been there all along; the thing is, we need the true Light to actually come in and give the seed the nourishment it needs to grow. Without Him, we will just keep searching for a temporary light source, and trust me, I have found that it never grows anything but temporary leaves that will wilt off.

Understanding the Light of God is crucial for us as children because we are His image-bearers. When we feel stuck in darkness, we need His light to come in. There comes a point where we must understand that once we know Him and allow Him in, His light then transfers into us. We as children become the light-bearers that penetrate atmospheres, communities, places, and people. That is the beauty of it. We can allow the darkness to pull us down, or we can stand firm in who we are and allow the true Light within us to radiate off us and change any room we walk into. I have found this is what we are often being called to do. When we feel like we are being pulled down, we must fight and stand firmly on the truth of who we are: the light carriers who walk into a room without allowing distractions, the darkness of sin, or the absence of God in a place to change us. We are the changers; we are the shifters of the atmosphere. The Light can't be put out because it's on the inside. This is powerful for us to grasp, and the beauty of being a child of God. As light carriers, people have the ability to see Christ Jesus in us as the Light of God shines through us.

It is these truths—that God is our Father, He is Love, and He is the Light that overcomes the darkness—that help us begin to understand the nature of our God. When we start digging deeper into His nature, a picture of who He truly is starts to come into play. We start to see His love for us, that He longs for us to see Him as our Father, that all along He has been redeeming His children's story to bring them back home; back to the communion found in the garden of Eden, before the Fall; the perfect picture of how God wanted it to look to walk in relationship and intimacy with Him.

It blows my mind that Yahweh, the Great I AM, wants a

relationship with me, and He calls me His daughter. It brings me to my knees in praise and thanks for His love for me. As I have begun to learn that everything about us is rooted in Him, and the more I see His true nature and character, the less I want to walk without Him.

You see, our identity can't be understood unless we begin to see God as a Daddy who longs to be in a relationship with His kids. What would be the point in seeking to understand our identity without understanding who our Creator is? We would walk around wondering if His plans were for us or against us, and we would spend countless anxious hours questioning things. It is once we begin to recognize when something is not in His nature that we can then begin to separate the truth from what is false, allowing us to see the very words that are spoken over us in a different light. We can then accept words that sound like Him and begin to peel off the words that were stuck to us that don't resemble His heart.

I was told by two different teachers growing up that I should never write because I was bad at writing papers. It was that word spoken over me that stuck, and every time I felt like I was supposed to write something, my excuse to the Lord was, "Well, I'm a bad writer, so I can't write that." I finally came face to face with that lie when writing this book. I heard the Lord say, "Who told you that? Those were not my words, and yet you have listened to them. Come, sit, and listen, to what my heart is really saying." Once I saw that those words I had believed about myself were a lie, I confessed it to the Lord and repented for coming into agreement with and speaking that lie over myself for all the years that I did. I then thanked Him that He saw something bigger in me than I saw in myself and asked

Him to show me what He saw in my writing. That is when He started to whisper His heart for my writing. This is what I mean when I say we need to start recognizing when words that are spoken over us do not line up with the nature of our loving Father and His heart for His children.

Three

Who is Jesus?

How would you describe Jesus? Many of us would say He is the perfect Son of God who died for our sins and rose again to give us life. Most of us would probably agree that He came not to judge us but to bring mercy and to rescue us from sin and death. Yet, I have found that there is so much more to Him than just this. He is a living and active member of the Trinity. A lot of times we blend Jesus and God in our minds, but He is actually his own individual person in the Trinity. Understanding that Jesus is God but that He is also distinct from the Father and the Holy Spirit has changed the way I see Him and interact with Him in prayer. I have learned what it is to walk in communion and relationship with Him. It is hard for me to put into words what He has done for me and how He has spoken life into my heart again and again since the dream in my testimony.

Before we can understand our own identity within the kingdom of God, there is something we must understand about Jesus: His presence transforms. One look in His eyes, and I was completely transformed. I saw Him so differently from how I had always viewed Him. In the midst of all the fear, doubt, and worry that I was battling, He was right there with me, not ashamed of me for struggling. I could see so much compassion, love, and tenderness in His eyes.

I saw something I had missed before: Jesus viewed me differently than I viewed myself. He could see my true heart, and He saw past the fear and anxious thoughts with no judgment or shame. I can't begin to even describe the emotions and the stirring in my spirit I felt at that moment. It was as if that one look touched deep down in my spirit, and now I can't go back to the before, nor do I want to. I want to describe in my best words who He is, what He has done, and what He continues to do. Jesus has literally transformed everything for us to be able to walk in freedom, authority, friendship with the Father, and to come into the heavenly places before the King in prayer.

So who is Jesus? Jesus Christ is our Redeemer. The story of the cross and His resurrection is true. I have seen how it transforms people, including me. He gently teaches us. He shows us, through His example in Scripture, how to be led by the Spirit of God and what it looks like to walk both in submission to and relationship with the Father. I have also seen Him as my Brother. He pushes me farther than I could ever go on my own, He runs alongside me, encouraging me to keep going. When I fall, He lifts me back up, brushes the dirt off me, and says, "You can do this. Eyes up," just like a big brother pushes a younger sibling, encouraging them to do their best, picking them up when they get knocked down.

Jesus the Firstborn

If we are sons and daughters of the Father, that would mean that Jesus, the Son of God, is our older brother. This is important to understand because part of knowing our identity is knowing our family and our inheritance. Romans 8:29 tells us Jesus is the firstborn of many brothers. Why is it important that He is the firstborn? The firstborn in Jewish culture played a significant role. It was law to dedicate the firstborn son to the Lord. As the first fruits of the womb (Exodus 13:12), firstborn sons would be an offering to the Lord, and they would receive a double inheritance. When Pharaoh refused to let the Israelites go, the Lord killed all of the firstborn sons in Egypt. The blood of lambs was painted over the Israelite doorways as a sign for the Spirit of the Lord to pass over their houses. The firstborns of the Israelites were redeemed by the lamb's blood. After the Lord led His people out of Egypt and gave them the law, He commanded that a firstborn lamb or animal be sacrificed to redeem the firstborn sons of the Israelites. Then, in Numbers 8:14-18 we see this shift:

Thus you shall separate the Levites from among the people of Israel, and the Levites shall be mine. And after that the Levites shall go in to serve at the tent of meeting, when you have cleansed them and offered them as a wave offering. For they are wholly given to me from among the people of Israel. Instead of all who open the womb, the firstborn of all the people of Israel, I have taken them for myself. For all the firstborn among the people of Israel are mine, both of man and of beast. On the day that I struck down all the firstborn in the land of Egypt I consecrated them for myself, and I have taken the Levites instead of all the firstborn among the people of Israel.

God takes the Levites as the firstborn sacrifice: consecrated, purified, and set apart to do His work. They stood in as the substitution for the firstborns of all Israel. In both of these laws, we can see a foreshadowing of the sacrifice of the Son of God. God gave His firstborn Son as the substitute for all the children of God. What a beautiful, prophetic picture intertwined throughout the Word of God.

Colossians 1:15, TPT, tells us that Jesus "is the divine portrait, the true likeness of the invisible God, and the firstborn heir of all creation." I touch on who we are because of Jesus in chapter five, but it is important for us to understand that as Jesus' brothers and sisters, we share in both His authority and His inheritance. However, as the firstborn, He holds the higher authority and the double inheritance: "...the firstborn heir in resurrection, He is the most exalted One, holding first place in everything" (Colossians 1:18, TPT). This means we are seated in heavenly places just as He is, yet He holds the highest honor by sitting at the right hand of God.

Jesus the Teacher

Throughout Mark 1, we often see references to Jesus's teaching or preaching. Jesus' core ministry was to teach, but His teaching was different from anything the people had heard before. Mark 1:22 says that "they were astonished at His teaching, for He taught them as one who had authority..." I believe this is important to understand because just as Jesus taught, He commanded us to also teach. As disciples of Jesus, we should also be able to teach with authority. Yet, there was something different about Jesus' teaching.

Jesus taught us kingdom principles and mindsets through parables. He taught us how to see and understand things in the heavenly realm by using earthly examples. We see Him do this throughout His narrative in the gospels. Through parables, He explained the principles of Heaven.

One of the most important things He taught while on earth was the heart of the Father. The people of God knew of His works, the signs and wonders He did, and His faithfulness to His people since the days of Noah, yet they saw God the Father as a harsh Judge. They had never fully experienced a relationship with Him. Part of Jesus' ministry was to show them the true heart of the Father, which so few people in the Old Testament had experienced. Abraham walked with God and was called His friend, Moses was also a friend of God, David was a man after God's own heart, Daniel spoke to Him and couldn't walk without Him, and Deborah listened and knew His voice in order to judge and give counsel to the people. There are many more who were mentioned in the Old Testament as having walked with God, but the people strayed so far, and their hearts hardened into legalism and worldliness, not understanding God's true heart. Jesus wanted the people He taught to see the true heart of His Father. He wanted them to understand that the Father wanted His children to know Him, that He saw them as His children.

It is crucial for us to understand Jesus' teachings because they point us to the ways of the Kingdom. They are blueprints of the Kingdom of God and how it works. The beauty of studying His teachings and the rest of Scripture is that each time we do, they still speak! Since the Word of God is living and active, and the Holy Spirit is at work within us to testify to what the Father is saying, He will often reveal more to us each time we read, even in very familiar passages. I love Psalm 119 because the words of the psalmist dig deep into why the teachings, commands, and testimonies of the Lord are so powerful: "Your marvelous words are living miracles, no wonder I long to obey everything you say. Break open your Word within me until revelation-light comes out! Those with open hearts are given insight into your plans" (Psalm 119:129-130, TPT). As we begin to break open His Word, a doorway is opened for us to step into a new understanding of who God is and how His kingdom works. Jesus is the doorway, and understanding the kingdom comes from reading His teachings and allowing the Spirit of God to breathe life in the words we read.

I want us to dig into some of these parables in the Gospels. There were several that Jesus actually interpreted for His disciples so they could begin to understand what He was saying. Mark 4:33-34, tells us Jesus always spoke in parables to the people, but in private, He explained them to His disciples. I believe it's important because often we see that, away from the crowd, the disciples would ask Him what He meant, and He would break it down more for them. I love that He responds to their hearts by giving them revelation. It often makes me think of what God told Jeremiah in 33:3, "Call to me and I will answer you, and will tell you great and hidden things that you have not known." We also see that it gave the disciples a basic understanding of the principles, mindsets, and teachings of the kingdom, which, along with the help and power of the Holy Spirit, would eventually help them to lead and teach others after He was gone.

In a sermon discussing Jesus' parables, Pastor Joshua Redding explained Jesus often uses the imagery of a sower in a field or a vineyard. It is important to note that in order to grow crops in the natural world, three things are needed: good soil, seed, and water. If the pH level of the soil is off or the soil is not porous enough to absorb water and easily provide oxygen and nutrients to the plants, the crops will not grow. I have been learning this while growing a garden with my children this year. This is why we see different regions yield certain crops better than others.

In Jesus' teachings, we must understand the soil represents our hearts. Just like good soil is porous, our hearts must be open so we can take in the living water and then give life (oxygen; aka God's breath, and nutrients; aka the Bread of Life or Word of God) to the fruit in our lives. The second thing needed to grow crops is the seed. The seed that is planted into the soil is the Word of God. Just as the growth of the seed depends on the nature of the soil, so the growth of fruit in our lives depends on the posture of our hearts. If our hearts are open, the seed will grow and bear fruit. Water is the third requirement for growing crops. Without water, the seed can dry out or wilt, bringing forth no crop. The "water" needed to grow the spiritual seed is the Holy Spirit. In order for us to grow and have life, we need the living water, which is the Spirit of God. I will go more in-depth about the Holy Spirit in the next chapter, but we see that even in Jesus' teaching, the Holy Spirit plays a key role in our growth and understanding.

I love this picture because of how it comes full circle. The disciples literally became the parable in reality. The parables they heard were the seeds Jesus was planting, the hearts open to learning and asking more questions were the fertile soil, and when the Holy Spirit fell, that was the water that caused the seeds to grow and bear fruit to the nations. As another layer, the disciples represent the children of God that have hearts that are fertile and sowable. The Church started small, but as the Word of God took root, it took His Church deeper and deeper into the soil, causing it to be anchored because of the living water (Holy Spirit) that gives it life. As it grows, it is then able to provide for and bring others in. As our branches grow (both individually and as the Church), we then have the ability to feed others through the fruit we bear, giving others rest and protection for the season and equipping others to also go out and make disciples.

This is where we have to learn to be taught from the Teacher Himself. We have to dig into the Word of God and ask the Holy Spirit to give us understanding and revelation of what the Father wants us to understand from a passage. It is when we begin to do this that we can then turn around and share it with those around us. When you start to see your Bible come to life, through the Spirit of God, it transforms everything for you. It is like a treasure hunt searching out the gems and diamonds that the Lord has laid before us, following the map that He has written out for us. I get excited every time He shows me something new, and I come with fresh eyes to read and be taught by Him. We must be willing to always be teachable, knowing that we are never above our teacher, the true Rabbi, who continues to teach us from the right hand of God.

Jesus the Redeemer

The Bible tells us in Romans 3:23, that "all have sinned and fall short of the glory of God." Sin entered the world when Eve and Adam disobeyed God and ate of the fruit of the tree of the knowledge of good and evil. Through their disobedience, the inheritance of sin for humanity entered the picture. "When Adam sinned, the entire world was affected. Sin entered human experience, and death was the result. And so death followed this sin, casting its shadow over all humanity, because all have sinned" (Romans 5:12, TPT). This is where our need for a Savior, or Redeemer, comes in. To redeem someone means to "buy back, repurchase, to free from captivity by payment or ransom; to release from blame or debt, to repair & restore."[3] This is what Jesus came to do. He came to buy us back, to free us from the captivity of sin, to release us from the blame and debt of sin over our lives, and to come into repair and restore what was broken because we could not redeem ourselves.

So, how did Jesus redeem us and what did it look like? For those who don't know, I want to share a story of love with you.

Jesus Christ, the Son of God, was born to a virgin named Mary in a lowly stable in Bethlehem. I would encourage you to read this story found in Luke 1:26-2:21. He is the true reason for Christmas, the celebration of the birth of a Savior. Jesus was born to Mary and Joseph, but He came from God to redeem and save us all. We see this in the life He lived while here on earth. Jesus walked in submission and obedience to His Heavenly Father. He walked the earth in the flesh, facing temptations just like we do, yet the Bible tells us He was without sin.

We see the heart of Jesus throughout the stories found in the Gospels: Matthew, Mark, Luke, and John. In the pages of these books, we see miracle after miracle, parable after parable, and teaching after teaching pointing us back to the truth. He spoke to people's hearts, having compassion on them, not sitting and placing judgment while speaking to them. When He spoke, it was with tenderness and love. He drew people out by speaking words of knowledge over them and then taking them to the truth of the Word. Thousands flocked to Him, following Him to see if what they heard was true. I believe that while many didn't leave disappointed, some did because they didn't truly see or hear what He was saying. They came for the miracles and healing, yet many often left not understanding that He had come to redeem and save them from themselves, not a Roman empire. He had been sent to redeem their story, to bring them into a relationship with the Father, and to be the sacrifice that would be accepted on the mercy seat once and for all.

In Luke 3:23, we see Jesus starting His ministry at thirty years of age. After being baptized by John the Baptist, He went into the wilderness where He fasted for forty days and nights before coming back and calling His disciples. We read in Mark 1:12, Jesus was led out to the wilderness by the Spirit. I believe that during Jesus' time in the wilderness, the Father spoke tenderly over Him as Jesus came to Him in prayer and fasting, God spoke life into Him, strengthening Him, and preparing Him for the three years that were ahead of Him. See, Jesus knew His time was short. He knew what the Father had called Him to do; that He would die as a living sacrifice.

He was fully God, but we have to remember He still lived in the flesh and was tempted in every way that we are. There had to be a mental battle in His mind to live and walk in the Spirit and not in his own flesh and emotions. Can you imagine the mental and emotional battles Jesus had to fight, knowing what was coming? I have no doubt Jesus had to wrestle with His mindset, knowing He was going to the cross. Paul would later go on to write about this very thing that Jesus showed us: taking every thought captive to obey Christ, who was obeying the Father (2 Corinthians 10:5-6).

Jesus continued forward with the plan that was set before Him. The beautiful thing about Jesus' story is that in the middle of all the healing, teaching, walking, and leading, He would often slip away just to be with the Father. This shows us the beauty of communion and the need we have for a relationship with God. He fills up our spirits. When we pour ourselves out for others, we need Him to fill us back up so that we can keep moving forward in His plan for us. This is what we see in Jesus. The Redeemer Himself needed time with the Father, even until the very end.

Jesus' ministry on earth lasted three years, and He knew He had much to do in that short time in the flesh. We see time and time again how He spoke without bringing shame or condemnation to the hearts of people and how He showed them their need for a true Savior. In the last two weeks of His life, we see how the atmosphere changed. People went from praising Him as He came into the city gates, crying, "Hosanna! Hosanna!" to shouting, "Crucify Him," just a week later. Why did they go from praising Him to calling for His crucifixion? The answer is because they didn't know they needed a Redeemer. They believed a Messiah was coming, but they thought the salvation He would bring was to rescue them from Roman oppression. They didn't recognize the Messiah when He came, and they didn't recognize the real salvation He was bringing—salvation from sin, death, and enslavement to the law. They didn't understand that Jesus came to redeem their spirits so they could have direct access to the Father.

Jesus knew He would be the ultimate sacrifice and the price to pay was His life. He also knew the freedom He bought for us that day would forever change things for humanity! What the crowd tried to do, under the hand of Satan, was kill Jesus, but what they didn't realize was that God had a bigger plan. As the Son of God hung on the cross, the Father poured out all of His wrath upon His Son. He literally turned His back on Jesus, abandoning Him, as every sin was placed upon Him. Jesus' blood is our redemption. What does this mean?

As I said above, "to redeem" means "to buy back." We originally belonged to the Father, but then, we were separated from Him because of the sin of Adam, which was passed down to every person. God gave the law as a way to atone for sins under the Old Covenant. But then Jesus came and established a New Covenant, buying us back with His blood so we could have freedom from sin, which meant freedom from the law. His blood redeemed us from the power of sin over us and of the penalty of our sin, which is death (Romans 6:23). The power of His blood gives us freedom from the dominion and reign of Satan, giving us back the authority that was originally given to us in the garden by God Himself in Genesis 1:26. In 1 Peter 1:18-19, it states that we "were ransomed from the futile ways inherited by our forefathers, not with anything perishable such as silver or gold, but with the precious blood of Christ, like that of a lamb without blemish or spot." So just as Adam brought the inheritance of sin, Jesus brought the inheritance of freedom from sin because His blood was the perfect sacrifice to restore us in relation with God the Father. This is what it looks like to walk as redeemed daughters of God.

Four

Who is the Holy Spirit?

*I have baptized you with water, but He
will baptize you with the Holy Spirit.*

Mark 1:8

*But the Helper, the Holy Spirit, whom the Father
will send in my name, He will teach you all things and
bring to your remembrance all that I have said to you.*

John 14:26

Who is the Holy Spirit? The Holy Spirit is the Spirit of God—
the third person in the Trinity. We know His name, but many
of us haven't been taught much about Him. He plays a role in
our relationship with Christ and in our identity as daughters
and sons of the Father, so it is imperative that we start with
understanding His role in the Trinity.

The Holy Spirit is often assumed to have first entered the
picture at Pentecost, but that is not the case at all. Genesis 1:2,
says, "The earth was without form and void and darkness was
over the face of the deep. And the Spirit of God was hovering
over the face of the waters." The Spirit of God has existed
since the beginning, and He always will exist. We read in 1

Thessalonians 5:23 that we are made of spirit, soul, and mind and everyone has a spirit that is eternal. This is a beautiful picture of how we are made in the image of our Father—we have a spirit just like He does. Yahweh, the one true God, sent His Spirit to come be with us and in us. This just blows my mind.

The Holy Spirit's role throughout Scripture changes, giving us particular insight into the many ways He works. In the Old Testament, we see that the Holy Spirit came upon people. In Numbers 24, the Spirit of God comes upon Balaam, filling His mouth with words to speak. In Exodus 31:2-5, God tells Moses that He will fill Bezalel *"with the Spirit of God, with ability and intelligence, etc."* in order to build the tabernacle. 1 Samuel 10:1-12, tells us that as the prophet Samuel anoints Saul as King of Israel, he gives him instructions and says that "when these signs meet you, do what your hand finds to do, for God is with you" (1 Samuel 10:7). As Saul leaves there and goes to where Samuel had instructed him to go, the Spirit of the Lord rushed upon him, and "God gave him another heart" (1 Samuel 10:9).

Throughout the Old Testament, we see the Spirit of the Lord coming upon people, filling their mouths to speak or their hands to do a specific task or carry out a particular purpose. The coming of the Holy Spirit appears in different ways: He gives a vision for the temple, empowers His people to build it, and is a primary way God speaks to his children. His purpose was to come and help the people do the work of God and lead them back to Him.

In the New Testament, the Holy Spirit plays a key role in Jesus' birth, ministry, and resurrection. We read in the first chapter of Matthew, Mary "was found to be with child from the Holy Spirit" (Matthew 1:18). Matthew 3:16, says that as Jesus was baptized and came up from the water, "the heavens were opened to Him, and He saw the Spirit of God descending like a dove and coming to rest on Him." We read of the presence of the Holy Spirit throughout Jesus' ministry. He was with Jesus during the forty days in the wilderness. His power was in Jesus as He taught, as He cast out demons, as He healed, and as He preached. He was with Him as He gave His life, and it was through the Holy Spirit that Jesus was raised from the dead.

From His birth to His death to His resurrection, the Holy Spirit was in and upon Jesus. The Holy Spirit was an active part of Jesus' ministry. He led Him, encouraged Him, and was with Him through everything. We see Jesus speaking to His disciples in John 14:16-17, 26: "And I will ask the Father, and He will give you another Helper, to be with you forever, even the Spirit of truth, whom the world cannot receive, because it neither sees Him nor knows Him. You know Him, for He dwells with you and will be in you...the Helper, the Holy Spirit, whom the Father will send in my name, He will teach you all things and bring to your remembrance all that I have said to you." Jesus promises His disciples the Holy Spirit will be the One to come and help lead them, speak truth to them, continue to teach them, and remind them of the things they had been taught.

Just before Jesus ascends into Heaven, He gives instructions to His disciples, telling them to "make disciples of all the nations, baptizing them in the name of the Father and of the Son and of the Holy Spirit, teaching them to observe all that I have commanded you" (Matthew 28:19-20). In Acts 1:4-5, while

Jesus was staying with His disciples, "He ordered them not to depart from Jerusalem, but to wait for the promise of the Father, which He said, 'you heard from me; for John baptized with water, but you will be baptized with the Holy Spirit not many days from now.'" It is the Holy Spirit who came as a rush of wind upon the disciples and those who were in the upper room on the day of Pentecost, and He is the one who would lead them in building the church as the Helper God had promised. He would be the One giving the believers of Jesus the power to walk in all that Jesus had commanded them to do in Matthew 28:19-20.

The Spirit of God is within us, leading us, encouraging us, and speaking truth to us. Often, we forget He is with us and is part of our story. The Holy Spirit plays a crucial role within us, declaring our identity over us, and leading us in how to walk in the ways of the Father. If we neglect to see Him or to understand His role, we neglect the Helper we have been given by the Father. Neglecting the Holy Spirit's guidance is like taking a road trip without a map or GPS. A friend of mine always says walking without Him is like driving a car without knowing where you're going and hoping to eventually arrive at the right destination. We would waste time and resources trying to find our way, and we could end up never arriving at our destination. Going through life without the Holy Spirit, we waste time, miss opportunities, run ourselves ragged, and may ultimately end up missing our destination.

Giver of Life

The Holy Spirit is the One who speaks life into our dry bones.

He is the One who calls us out of the emptiness of our souls. He speaks to our spirits and calls us by name. God's Spirit aligns with ours, bringing life in the spiritual realm. John 6:63 says, "It is the Spirit who gives life; the flesh is no help at all." Jesus' blood was poured out for us so the Spirit of God could be poured out on us, making us temples of the living God. His Spirit dwells in those of us who have called upon the name of the Lord, giving us new life.

What does this mean for us? It means that our bodies, minds, and emotions are called to life. As the Spirit pours into us, our spirit comes alive—whole and renewed, flowing forth with the life of Heaven. Yet, as we still walk this earth, we know our flesh and our minds struggle because sin and darkness are present. But the Spirit of God is calling us to come to the Father with pure hands and hearts, consecrated and set apart for His glory. It is the Holy Spirit who comes into us, restoring the broken parts of us, renewing our skewed mindsets, and redeeming the agreements we have made, even unknowingly, with the enemy.

The Holy Spirit steps in and begins to heal from the inside out, and our spirits begin to fall into alignment with what He is doing in us. Luke 6:45 says, "The good person out of the good treasure of his heart produces good, and the evil person out of his evil treasure produces evil, for out of the abundance of the heart his mouth speaks." As our hearts begin to be restored and set in kingdom ways, our mouths will speak words of life and not death. Instead of words of brokenness, uncertainty, or emptiness—words of healing, courage, and peace. Where there was once spiritual barrenness in our homes and communities, life is now birthed because of the Holy Spirit's healing work in our lives.

The Holy Spirit can have a tangible impact on us if we let Him. Many times, we get in our way by ignoring Him or squelching the fire inside of us. If we allowed Him to be real to us, our healing would be so much more fruitful. This fruitfulness then would spill over into the lives of those around us. Can you imagine? As we allow the Holy Spirit to pour life and alignment into us, it will spill over into our homes, our schools, our neighborhoods, and our communities. There is no limit to the impact of the Holy Spirit as we offer ourselves in faith to be used by Him. This is what we were created for. We were created to speak and give life. We have to let the Spirit of God come in and realign us to the heart of the Father.

As we begin to participate with the Holy Spirit, our perspective changes. When we let Him take over, we no longer fall for the old things that used to tempt us. As our muscles begin to stretch, we become stronger. The old lens through which we saw the world starts to fall off as our eyes are restored to how we were originally created to see the world. We find wholeness in Him. We're not meant to wait until heaven to see these things become a reality; it is meant to start now, even amidst the brokenness. Do you see it? It's Isaiah 61:1-3 that says, "the Spirit of God is upon [us], because the Lord has anointed [us] to bring good news to the poor; He has called [us] to bind up the brokenhearted, to proclaim liberty to the captives, and the opening of the prison to those who are bound...to comfort those who mourn, to grant those who mourn...the oil of gladness instead of mourning, the garment of praise instead of a faint spirit." We have also been called to do the very thing Jesus prophesied that He was sent to do.

However, we have a problem. If we are to walk like Jesus did—setting captives free, proclaiming liberty, allowing those who mourn to see the truth so they can rejoice and walk in garments of praise—then we have to allow the Holy Spirit to step in and do His work. You see, we were born spiritually dead and with a broken root system. Our roots need a source of life, and if they are not planted in life-giving soil we will eventually rot, and all joy, peace, and love will be choked out. This is where the Life-giver steps in and starts to pull out those entangled, rotting roots. The Holy Spirit is what brings life, so if we neglect Him, we neglect the most vital part of growing our roots. He stirs up the soil, adding the things needed to make it fertile and life-giving for fruitfulness.

It is the glory of God to have us planted with our roots deep into the ground. We read in Isaiah 61:3, "that they may be called oaks of righteousness, the planting of the Lord, that He may be glorified." The Lord is the one who plants us so we can grow to be strong oaks of righteousness. If you have never seen an oak tree, they become very large and tall. Their roots begin to take over the ground and run deep. I have oak trees in my yard, and we often mow over the massive roots because they stick out of the ground. What amazes me is how widely they spread out from the tree itself.

Not only do their roots grow deep, but they grow wide, taking the area around them. What a beautiful picture of how the Lord grows us. It is impossible to grow into oaks of righteousness if we don't allow the Holy Spirit to come in and speak life into the areas within us that are causing decay. We desperately need the Spirit to give us life. It is so vital to our survival. If we are going to understand who we are, we need to know who the Holy Spirit is and welcome Him in to give us life. Trust me, when we allow Him to come in and start to give life to the areas of our lives that have kept us entangled in sin and darkness, it is His joy to step in, redeem and restore those areas for us. Sometimes the process is painful, but it is needed. In the end, we are the ones who step out full, whole, restored, and prepared to bring fruit to our surroundings.

The righteous flourish like the palm tree and grow like
a cedar in Lebanon. They are planted in the house
of the Lord; they flourish in the courts of our God.
They still bear fruit in old age; they are ever full
of sap and green, to declare that the Lord is upright;
he is my rock, and there is no unrighteousness in him.

Psalm 92:12-15

Spirit of Truth

But when the Helper comes, whom I will send to
you from the Father, the Spirit of truth, who
proceeds from the Father, He will bear
witness about me. He bears witness to the truth.

John 15:26

The Greek word for the phrase "bear witness" is the word "martyreō." It means "to affirm that one has seen or heard or experienced something; to testify; to give and not keep back testimony."[4] The Holy Spirit is the one who affirms who Jesus is and all that He has done. He testifies to the divine revelation and inspiration that comes through both the written and spoken word of God.

In order to testify or to affirm something, one must have experienced or seen it firsthand. This points us to the beauty of the Trinity. The members of the Trinity can testify to one another because they have each seen firsthand what the others have done. Jesus tells us that "when the Helper comes, whom I will send to you from the Father, the Spirit of truth, who proceeds from the Father, He will bear witness about me" (John 15:26). We also read in 1 John 5:7-10 (TPT), "So we have these three constant witnesses giving their evidence: the Spirit, the water, and the blood. And these three are in agreement. If we accept the testimony of men, how much more should we accept the more authoritative testimony of God that He has testified concerning His Son? Those who believe in the Son of God have the living testimony in their hearts. Those who don't believe have made God out to be a liar by not believing the testimony God has confirmed about his Son." The Holy Spirit sees and knows what the Father is doing and then testifies to it. Those who have believed in Jesus, we walk with this "living testimony," the Holy Spirit, within us. This leaves us with the question: How does He testify what the Father is doing or saying to us?

There are numerous ways the Holy Spirit speaks. He can speak through creation, a still small voice, dreams, visions, prophecies, or our consciences. What is important to understand is He is speaking! Jesus says in John 16:12-13, "I still have many things to say to you, but you cannot bear them now. When the Spirit of truth comes, He will guide you into all the truth." If the Bible quotes Jesus as saying there is more for us to know and the Holy Spirit will reveal it, then we must take this seriously and not limit who we think God is and what we think He does and says. He is so much bigger! We must know

Him, not just know *about* Him. Only then will we be able to truly recognize His voice in the midst of the clamor of other voices. In John 10, Jesus tells a parable in which a shepherd calls his sheep. He says they follow the shepherd because they know his voice. He interprets the parable and says in verse 14, "I am the good shepherd. I know my own and my own know me…" We must *know* His voice. We must know *Him*.

We must learn to be still and listen to what He is saying, remembering that when He speaks, His words are words of life—straight from the Father. It is in the stillness that He often speaks, yet we have become so distracted by the noise around us that we often miss His voice. I can testify, from experience, that it is most often in the stillness and quiet that I have heard Him, just like when He came before Elijah. He wasn't in the fire, the earthquake, or the wind, but a still small voice (1 Kings 19:11-13). This is why we have to learn to sit and just be still. Don't get me wrong; He can speak through the other things, but most often, you will find when the Spirit speaks to you, it is in the quiet place when you are open to receiving what He is saying. It is when I'm sitting in His presence with my heart open to receive that He begins to speak, and I begin to write. Other times, it has been in moments of worship, prayer, or gathering with other believers where He begins to speak or show me things that are on His heart. Why? I believe it is because God earnestly loves to speak to those who seek Him.

This is why, as sons and daughters of God, it is important to invite the Holy Spirit into our daily lives and to ask Him what He is saying. You can ask Him to speak to you and help you discern whether it is His voice you are hearing or another voice. Test what you hear, just like 1 John 4:1 says, "Beloved, do not believe every spirit, but test the spirits to see whether they are from God." Do not be afraid to ask Him to confirm His words to you. When you're first starting out learning to hear and recognize His voice, I encourage you to step out in little acts of faith and try doing what you think you heard, making sure it aligns with Scripture and the Father's heart. The Holy Spirit is a gentle guide, and He will lead you into all truth. The Father knows your heart, and as you press into Him, He will draw near to you. Ask and keep on asking. Let your faith rise and your desire for Him grow. Remember His promise: "Afterwards I will give them this covenant: I will embed my laws into their hearts and fasten my Word to their thoughts" (Hebrews 10:16, TPT).

The Holy Spirit is the Spirit of Truth that comes to dwell within us when we place our trust in all that Jesus did on the cross. We can call out in faith to Him as our one true God. Although we have the Holy Spirit, there are still things that are hard to grasp and apply to our lives. One example I struggle with is miracles and healings. This is because I have often brought my own medical understanding to try to perceive. My natural understanding has often been my biggest stumbling block. 1 Corinthians 2:10 says, "...these things God has revealed to us through the Spirit. For the Spirit searches everything, even the depths of God."

See, when we open up our minds, hearts, and spirits to allow the Spirit of God to speak, we begin to see and understand things that don't make sense in the natural world. Paul says that the "natural person does not accept the things of the Spirit of God, for they are folly to him" (1 Corinthians 2:14). The things of the Spirit are spiritually discerned. When we begin to walk by the Spirit, the things that don't make sense will start to be our normal. When we allow ourselves to be fully open to the things of the Holy Spirit, making room for Him to move and speak, that is when the Spirit begins to reveal more mysteries and revelations of the Father.

Mighty Counselor

For all who are led by the Spirit of God are sons of God.

Romans 8:14

The Spirit of God is the one who should lead us. Romans 8, repeatedly tells us that to live and walk by the flesh is death, but to live and walk by the Spirit is life. What does this mean? It means that we live according to what the Spirit says to be true. To do this, we must first be aware of His voice and how He speaks to us. He is the one who intercedes on our behalfs, according to the Father's will (Romans 8:27). As I said above, He speaks in different ways, so we must ask the Father for ears to hear His voice and be open and humble enough to listen when He speaks.

In the last few years, I have been praying for the Lord to reveal Himself more to me through His Spirit. I want the Holy Spirit to be more real to me than the clothes that I wear. I feel like He has been showing me the importance of His Spirit as I have been reading the New Testament. I am still learning to be fully led by the Holy Spirit, but I can attest that time and time again, when I have chosen to listen to and follow Him, it has been beyond worth it, and He has poured out His blessings. Sometimes, the blessings are just for me, and other times, I get to witness Him blessing others through me. As I step out in obedience and faith to pray for them or to speak words over them that He has given me, I can encourage and bring life to others.

I experienced this at the beginning of 2020. In 2019, my husband and I began praying over his career. He was working a 9-5 job while also running his own business in the evenings. As we took this before the Father in prayer and fasting, we began to hear the same answer: Jason was to leave his job and run his business full-time. We began to pray about what that would look like for him and for our family. We felt the Spirit giving us instructions for the next steps to take. In January of 2020, Jason gave notice to leave the job where he had worked for over a decade. What I haven't told you yet is he had just received a promotion the year before. What didn't make sense to many around us made sense to us spiritually as we obeyed God. He was doing something more than we could have imagined. Two months later, the whole world seemed to come to a halt overnight, including the industry Jason had just left. Looking back, we know this was the Lord's way of protecting our family and moving us into a new season. That first year running his business full-time, Jason received more business than we could have dreamed. This has been just one of the blessings of following the Spirit of God and obeying even when it didn't make sense.

It is important to talk about the word "blessings," as we use it so often in the church, and people often automatically assume blessings are finances. While in this story, obedience led to our finances being blessed, there have been many other times where the blessing of walking in obedience came in joyfulness, peace in a situation, or just the blessing of Him being near. Sometimes, the blessings are tangible, and sometimes they are not, but in my experience, however, when God chooses to pour out His blessings, it is always sweet.

When we begin to recognize the Spirit's voice, following His prompting becomes part of the everyday adventure. Walking with Him leading is extraordinary. Christian author, minister, and evangelist Bill Johnson once said, "The Holy Spirit is with you to lead you, but He comes upon you for someone else."[5] What this means for Spirit-led children of God is that as we walk, we are fully aware and in tune to what the Holy Spirit is continually speaking to us. We carry the aroma of Heaven because we are seated in heavenly places. If we are tuned in to Heaven and the kingdom, then we are going to be influenced by that atmosphere, and it will be evident in our lives. To be alive in the Spirit is being sensitive to the things of the spirit realm. We know that the world in which we live and breathe is our temporary home, and it is influenced by the spiritual realm. When we begin to live with an awareness of the spiritual realm, we begin to see others differently because we see that spirits, both good and evil, influence the environment around us. As the Spirit leads us, He often reveals things to us we have never seen before without Him.

I once heard an acquaintance of mine was suffering from a particular medical condition. Because of my nursing background, I knew all about the diagnosis and disease progression of the person, yet the Holy Spirit kept saying, "There is more than what you think." As I prayed, He began to show me the medical diagnosis was not what appeared in the natural world but rather a demonic entity that was mimicking natural symptoms of a disease. My friend, who also was a nurse, and I felt like we were being called to pray and ask the Holy Spirit for his eyes to see what was going on. As we prayed and asked for revelation of the situation, I remember Him showing me an image in worship of what was going on and what we were called to address. My friend, the nurse, who was close to the family, was literally at the hospital when I called her. She was able to lay hands on Him and speak life over Him, as she allowed the Spirit to lead her words and rebuke what the Holy Spirit showed us. Our faith was stirred. Days later, what looked in the natural world to be an awful scenario, the Lord did the exact opposite, and our friend woke up and was discharged a week later from the ICU. We both knew in our spirits the very thing we had interceded for was the very reason we saw this miracle life walk out of the hospital. I knew then that the Holy Spirit was beginning to show me the things I see with my natural "fleshly" eyes are not always what they seem.

Learning to be led first by the Spirit, rather than by my medical knowledge, is a constant journey. At times, I have allowed my medical understanding to hinder me from being able to ask what the Lord wants to do and to listen attentively to His voice. But the times when I have listened and then obeyed what He speaks to me, I have seen him move in miraculous ways. I have been in moments of worship or in prayer with others, and I have received a nudge in my spirit, often a picture, movie-like image, or even a small voice speaking to me about someone near me. In most cases when I have conquered my fear of speaking to them, I have gone over and spoken what He asked me to. This has usually started a conversation and turned into the Spirit encouraging them, my praying over them, or them realizing God sees them and hears them. While I often never see the outcome because I was just a messenger, it stirs my faith and heart to see Him move more, and my own thoughts and fears move aside as He leads me.

There have been times where He has given me a dream or a word for someone that I haven't spoken to in a while, and He has placed it on my heart to either intercede for them or just pick up the phone and reach out. Often, the response I receive when I call is, "How did you know to call, and how did you know that?" I don't say this to toot my own horn but to give you examples of what it looks like to listen and follow His lead. We might never know the full power of obeying what He tells us to do, but I do know that whether or not I know this side of Heaven, I want Him to say I obeyed and not ask me why I didn't.

I believe this is important for us to understand if we are going to be sons and daughters who walk by the Spirit. We must not become focused on the way things appear in the natural world because He will often ask us to speak up and address something in the spiritual realm that is really the cause of what we're observing around us. This has been the adventurous part of learning to walk by the Spirit and allowing Him to lead me. My hope is we become more aware of the ways the Father is asking us to step into the role of His daughter or son and to see Him for who He really is.

Pray this with me: "Father, give us eyes to see what you are doing! Holy Spirit, lead us in how to walk, being led by you. Let us have ears to hear the gentle whisper and nudges you give to us that we may walk according to your Word. Let us not get in the way of what you are doing in our lives but be obedient and humble, so you can come in and do what you do best—remove the broken root systems and replace them with life-giving ones. Oh Lord, make us more like your Son Jesus, who was obedient even to the point of death. Let us be lights that shine brightly into this dark world, for we carry the power of your Spirit, God, within us!"

Five

Now: Who Are You?

What does it look like to walk in spiritual blessings? As I asked the Lord this, He began to show me both what it looks like for us to walk in spiritual blessings and what it looks like to walk without them. Knowing what our inheritance is plays a key role in how we walk.

Let's say I inherited millions of dollars from a deceased uncle who lived overseas, and I was unaware this money sat in a bank in another country with my name on it. I would continue to go about my daily routine, having no idea I had so much to lose. But what if I got word about this fortune that was left to me—all I had to do was go sign a paper, and it would belong to me? I can tell you I would find a way to get overseas and sign that paper.

That's how it is with our spiritual blessings and inheritance. Many of us have no idea what we have been given as sons and daughters of the King and how we are seen by Him. We so often walk around as though we are powerless or defeated because we don't realize there is so much more to what Jesus has done for us than granting us access to Heaven when we die. I know that I did not understand the spiritual blessings that I had been freely given as an inheritance, through the blood of

Jesus.

I could quote you the verse below about our inheritance; I had head knowledge about it, but heart knowledge and head knowledge are quite different. After my encounter with Jesus, the Holy Spirit began to show me all that I had been given through the precious blood sacrifice poured out for me. This made me all the more eager to sit and listen to His direction, searching out more and beginning to walk in the calling, identity, and purpose Jesus called me to and for which He died. I believe this is what Paul wanted the church in Ephesus to understand. He knew all they would miss out on if they didn't understand their own blessings.

Blessed be the God and Father of our Lord Jesus Christ, who has blessed us in Christ with every spiritual blessing in the heavenly places, even as He chose us in Him before the foundation of the world, that we should be holy and blameless before Him. In love He predestined us for adoption to Himself as sons through Jesus Christ, according to the purpose of His will, to the praise of His glorious grace, with which He has blessed us in the Beloved. In Him we have redemption through His blood, the forgiveness of our trespasses, according to the riches of his grace, which He lavished upon us, in all wisdom and insight making known to us the mystery of His will, according to His purpose, which He set forth in Christ as a plan for the fullness of time, to unite all things in Him, things in heaven and things on earth. In Him we have obtained an inheritance, having been predestined according to the purpose of Him who works all things according to the counsel of His will, so that we who were the first to hope in Christ might be to the praise of His glory. In Him you also, when you heard the word of truth, the gospel of your salvation, and believed in Him, were sealed with the promised Holy Spirit, who is the guarantee of our inheritance until we acquire possession of it, to the praise of His glory.

Ephesians 1:3-14

Heirs to the Throne (Daughters/Sons)

Ephesians 5:4-5, tells us it is God's love for us that predestined us for adoption as sons and daughters because of the blood of Jesus. From the beginning, we were set apart from all of God's creation (including all spiritual beings) to be called His children. God, Himself, created us in His own image, making us unlike anything else that existed. He wanted us to be His image-bearers.

For me, this concept of being His daughter was a hard one to understand. I couldn't wrap my head around the fact that God actually wanted me to be His daughter and that's truly how He sees me. I didn't see myself as lovable at times, and I struggled with the feeling I didn't deserve His love because of things in my past. But that is the thing: I don't deserve His love, still, He loves me regardless and wants me as His own. There is nothing I could do to screw it up, and nothing could separate me from Him. He calls me His own. He began to show me how I was His daughter and to speak of what it truly meant to be called His.

We are daughters and heiresses to an everlasting throne...I mean, isn't it every little girl's dream to be a princess? I think, deep down, we have this desire and longing to be loved, treasured, and given a place of honor because it was placed within us from the time we were born. If we are image-bearers of God, then, there must be something inside of us that longs to walk in what we were created for. It's just like in the movies when the ordinary girl ends up finding out she's a princess in some foreign country. It is true! We literally have been adopted to walk in an eternal inheritance as daughters of an everlasting throne that will never be overthrown.

[I] will be a father to you, and you shall be sons and daughters to me, says the Lord Almighty.

2 Corinthians 6:1

Walking as a daughter means we get to be in a relationship and commune with Him, living as heirs of an inheritance and knowing what He has spoken over us is true. As a daughter of God, who knows who I am, I can trust my Father is good because I recognize His nature. I am now confident that what He plans for me is good, He sees the best in me, and His heart is to draw out what He put in me for His greater purpose. How do I know this? Because I have experienced it firsthand. As I shared previously about my senior year, I did not see Him as a good Father. I saw Him as harsh and as a disciplinarian more than someone who loved and cared for me.

I can't recall the exact moment it all changed, but I do know that after five or six years of walking in my own way, I never felt more loved than when I realized He had been there all along. In the midst of my waywardness, partying, and trying to find happiness in the things of the world, He was there with me and had been all along; I just didn't realize it was Him. I look back and remember so many times when I had been drinking and partying with friends having no idea how I got home. One night, in particular, I had been drinking at a frat party in a cornfield, and it was busted by the cops. My roommate and I ran through the cornfield and ended up running into an electric fence. We were shocked by it, but looking back, we should have gotten hurt worse.

There were so many times I could have been and probably was in true danger, but I know the Lord placed protection over me. Years later, I found out from my former pastor's wife that she had felt the need many times to get up at night and pray for me. To this day, it brings me to tears—to know that even in my running away, His heart was for me, and He really had been chasing me all that time. I could go on and on with stories of how He has proven His kindness and goodness in my life.

As a daughter, I know the power and authority my Father holds, and because I am His and His Spirit is within me, I have access to this power and authority as well. I walk and carry out what my Father, the King, says and does. His heart for His children is loving, kind, and full of mercy. I know His heart is for His kids to see Him for who He really is and to see the purpose for which they were created. But the best part is He knows me by name, as His daughter. He calls each one of us by our given name and knows everything about us. He knows the worst parts of us yet still calls us His daughters and sons. God has never been ashamed of us as His children. He boldly boasts He is with us wherever we go! His Word states He goes before us, behind us, and is all around us (Psalm 139:5, NLT). We are His children, and He longs for us to know and understand our identity and what we were created for.

Redemption & Forgiveness

I talked previously about Jesus as our Redeemer, but I want to go more in-depth with what it means to be redeemed and bought by the blood of Jesus. We must understand the power of Jesus' blood and all He redeemed us from in order to understand our identity as daughters and sons and all that has been given to us as a result. I knew His blood purchased our freedom and the right to go to Heaven, but I'm beginning to see and learn there is much more to it than that.

When we say we have been redeemed by the blood of the Lamb, this means we have been redeemed from the power that sin has over us, and we have been set free. We were once slaves to sin—shackled to it—but Jesus' blood breaks the chains off and declares us free to walk with Him. The reign of sin over us has ended. Now that we are covered in the blood of Jesus, our guilty consciences and condemnation that came with the penalty of our sin are broken off, and the grip and dominion Satan had to rule us is no more. Instead, as James 4:7, says, we have the freedom to walk away from sin and to resist the devil because we have submitted ourselves to God. We don't walk around as condemned slaves to sin but as holy and righteous servants of the Lord because we are seen in the light of the cross. The Bible says we are no longer condemned because we belong in Christ Jesus and have been set free from the law of death and sin (Romans 8:1-2).

Walking in the light of our redemption means we get to walk as children of God, not as slaves (Galatians 4:7). We have to know we are set free in order to walk in freedom, right? Picture the door of a jail cell that has been unlocked, but the prisoner doesn't know it is unlocked and he can go free. This is the case for so many sons and daughters today. They live as if they are still slaves to their sin and to the rule of Satan in their lives because they don't truly understand they have been set free and now have the power and authority to resist the devil because of the blood of Jesus. Yet, the Bible clearly says we do! This is the best news ever! It means we get to walk in freedom—freedom from condemnation and guilt, freedom from the grip of Satan's dominion, and freedom from guilty consciences.

We can have the freedom to walk in the will of God, live out our God-given purpose, and operate in the authority that was given to us at the beginning of creation. We get the freedom to have a relationship with the Father and to walk in intimacy with Him. We are free from having to bring sacrifices and burnt offerings to atone for our sins. We have the freedom to walk in emotional, physical, and spiritual healing because of the blood of Jesus that was shed for us. This is what it looks like to walk as forgiven and redeemed children.

We have been forgiven through the process of redemption. The Bible tells us "without the shedding of blood there is no forgiveness of sins" (Hebrews 9:22). Jesus literally had to bleed out in accordance with the law so we might be forgiven and set free. This means we get to walk in the forgiveness of every past, present, and future sin because of the blood of Jesus. His blood has the authority and power to wipe the slate clean, casting away our sin and remembering it no more. Isaiah 43:25, says, "I, even I, am He who blots out your transgressions for my own sake, and I will not remember your sins." In Romans 8:1, Paul writes, "there is now no condemnation for those who are in Christ Jesus." God does not hold our sins against us, for when He sees us, He sees Jesus. Like I mentioned in my testimony at the beginning of this book, I used to buy into the lie that my past sins were being held over me. But as we have seen, this is not the heart of the Father. Scripture tells us, "If we confess our sins, He is faithful and just to forgive us our sins and to cleanse us from all unrighteousness" (1 John 1:9).

Many of us get lost in the lie only because we can't forgive ourselves. We place condemnation, shame, and guilt on ourselves, allowing it to swallow us up in the belief that what we did can never be forgiven or that our wrongs will be held against us. The Bible tells us that is not true; in fact, it is quite the opposite. We have been forgiven, and our sins will not be held against us. God's Word says our sins will no longer be remembered. All we have to do is confess to them. And even confessing our sins is not a scary or burdensome task because there is no condemnation or shame for us any longer! How freeing is that? I know when I started to truly understand and walk in the light of that truth, it set me free from the things I'd held over myself. It set me free to walk in my spiritual blessing of being forgiven and redeemed and of not being enslaved to my sin and my past. The question is: Can you accept this truth and allow yourself to walk in freedom?

What does this look like practically? In my life, it looks like me speaking the truth in the face of condemning thoughts, declaring I have been redeemed and set free from the rule of condemnation and I am a daughter now, in right-standing before my Father. I then confess to Jesus any area where I have fallen short and lay it at His feet, saying aloud: "Jesus, I know I was bought with the high price of your blood, and the enemy is coming in and condemning me. I feel heavy with guilt and shame, but I know your Word says you have set me free from that. So, I thank you that I have been redeemed and set free by your blood today. I lay these lying thoughts at your feet and thank you that you took all my condemnation upon yourself." You see, this is what we as daughters and sons get to do—we get to stand and declare we have been covered and forgiven and then live in the freedom of that truth.

Holy & Blameless

Because our spirits have been born again, this means they have been made new by the blood of Jesus. We are holy, blameless, and above reproach (Colossians 1:21-22), righteous in the sight of the Father.

So now the case is closed. There remains no accusing voice of condemnation against those who are joined in life-union with Jesus, the Anointed One.

Romans 8:1, TPT

Revelation 12:10-12, tells us the accuser comes before Him to accuse the sons of man day and night. I picture God the Father seated in the courtroom of Heaven as the Devil brings his accusations. But the blood of Jesus has power! You see, those who believe and have confessed that Jesus is the Son of God are holy, righteous, and blameless, so as Satan attempts to make a case against us in the courtroom, Jesus gets up and intercedes for us. As God, the Judge of the courtroom, looks over at us, He sees not our sins but His Son. He sees the Holy One—the perfect, spotless lamb of God. As God looks at His Son, He recalls the stripes Jesus incurred for us; He sees the holes in Jesus' hands, feet, and side. He knows this is His beloved Son who took all the Father's wrath upon himself to rescue His children. This is He, Christ Jesus, who went down to hell and recovered authority from the enemy, and then rose again on the third day, taking victory over death and the law. When God looks at His daughters and sons, He sees Jesus, the firstborn of many.

This is what it looks like to be holy, righteous, and blameless. We are imputed with these attributes and statuses, meaning we did absolutely nothing to earn them. All we are called to do is to place our faith in the One who redeemed the story. What a beautiful gift we have been given as an inheritance because of Jesus' blood!

Beloved

What does it mean to be beloved? In Greek, the word for "beloved" is "agapao"[6] meaning "to love." In the Bible, it's the love with which God regards Christ Jesus, His firstborn Son (Ephesians 1:6). God holds this love for all His sons and daughters. As we begin to see ourselves as adopted children of God, we will see this "agapao" love is being poured out upon us too. This spiritual blessing is important because it changes the way we view ourselves. We are commanded eight times in the Bible to love our neighbor as we love ourselves. I believe we must understand how loved we are by God and start seeing ourselves through His eyes in order to grasp the idea we are called to love even ourselves. We're not told to love our neighbors *instead* of ourselves but *as* we love ourselves.

Now: Who Are You?

Why is it so hard for most of us to love ourselves or see ourselves as lovable?

Many of us struggle to love ourselves or to see ourselves as beloved because we carry shame from our pasts—things done to us or things we chose to do. Lies from the enemy about who we are by way of unkind words that have been spoken over us, can also cause us to not love ourselves. Some of us have even been told directly we are unloveable, and we believed it. Others may have never been shown true love, particularly by those who were supposed to love us, like our parents or our spouses. Many who grew up in the church may find it hard to love themselves because of direct or implied teaching that loving oneself is prideful, selfish, or is exalting oneself above the Lord. This religious mindset can cause us to walk around thinking we are undeserving of God's love and of anything He has put on our hearts. I have struggled with this, and I have known people who think the very fact that they desire something means they have to deny themselves in order to be godly. There are many different tactics the enemy uses to cause us not to be able to love ourselves or see ourselves as loved, including belittling the importance of either. These lies that say loving ourselves or believing we're loved are not important are a direct attack on our identity as beloved sons and daughters of God.

If Jesus Christ gave up His own life for us because of His love of the Father, why would we turn around and snub what He declares is lovely? We are called temples of the Holy Spirit, a royal priesthood, a people for His own possession, beloved children, servants of the Most High, brothers and co-heirs with Christ—we are highly valued by the King of Kings, so we must not diminish our value by not loving what He loves, including ourselves. When our view of ourselves does not line up with God's view of us, we have an orphan mindset. We long to feel loved and to truly be loved, but we do not feel worthy. The Bible is very clear that we are not orphans but beloved sons and daughters of God.

Today, I want to break off that lie that has kept you chained down and unable to receive love because Scripture says God loved us before we were even created. The Bible tells us "that neither death nor life, nor angels nor rulers, nor things present nor things to come, nor powers, nor height nor depth, nor anything else in all creation, will be able to separate us from the love of God in Christ Jesus our Lord" (Romans 8:38-39). So, whatever we have done that makes us think we are unloveable, the truth is it can't keep us from the love of God. It won't separate us, and it doesn't cause Him to be ashamed of or embarrassed by us. Rather, God the Father says: "Draw close, let me hold you; for I am the One who loves you, and nothing will separate you from my love."

When we allow ourselves to be loved and held by Him, we are then able to break through the barriers that keep us from loving others. When God started addressing this in my life, I had to let my walls down and let the Father's love rush in. Growing up, I often felt criticized, judged, and held under a microscope by people in my life who pointed out all of my flaws. I internalized what they said, let their words shape my view of my identity, and then pushed them away angry and bitter. I would become very easily agitated with them and couldn't stand to be around them. Every time I felt that way, I would begin to declare out loud I am beloved by the One who created everything. Yahweh, the Great I Am, loved me before I was even born.

Now that I know who I truly am as a beloved daughter of God, the words of other people don't carry the weight they once did. All I really care about is what He says of me. When people come against me with criticism or judgments, I find I am able to let go of offense quickly and let the love of the Father speak over the situation and flow through me back to them. My flesh may want to respond with agitation or defensive words, but the more I feed my spirit with God's love, the more I am able to truly repay evil with good from a genuine and transformed heart. Now, instead of becoming bitter, I am able to love. Only He has a perfect love—a love that doesn't come with conditions or terms but is freely given with no strings attached. This is the perfect love that has been given to us. Many of us just need to receive it and let it break down our walls. His love changes everything!

Seated in Heavenly Places

Ephesians 2:6, says God has "raised us up with Christ and seated us with Him in heavenly places." What does this mean exactly? Well, in order to begin to understand this, we must first see every person is made up of body, soul, and spirit. Our body and soul are things we are very aware of and tuned into, yet many of us are often unsure of what our spirit really is. This is important for us to grasp. Each one of us has a spirit, according to Scripture, yet it is the only part of us we cannot literally sense in a natural way. This makes it hard to understand when our minds can't sense its presence. One's spirit is what is eternal. It is the thing we often hear spoken of when people ask what happens when we die. The terms "spirit" and "soul" are often used interchangeably, so I found it helpful to learn the Greek word for "soul" in the context of this verse. "Body, soul, and spirit," referred to by Paul, actually translates to *"psyche,"*[7] which means "the breath that gives life to a man/animal; the seat of the feelings, desires, emotions, affections, and aversions - our heart." The word "spirit," used by Paul, in 1 Thessalonians 5:23, is the Greek word *"pneuma,"*[8] meaning "the rational part of man; the power of perceiving and grasping divine and eternal things, and upon which the Spirit of God exerts its influence."

Just as God Himself has a spirit, who we know as the Holy Spirit, so we have a spirit. It is the part of us that lives in the spiritual realm, which is literally all around us. We are told in Ephesians 6:12, our battle isn't against flesh and blood but against the cosmic forces of darkness in the heavenly realms. In the spiritual realm, there are angels, demons, and living spirits. When you become redeemed by the blood of Jesus, your living spirit is actually seated in the heavenly places. This means you have access to the heavenly realm anytime you want. I know this sounds confusing, and it is if we try to perceive with our natural minds, but the more we press into the Spirit for revelation, the more He reveals how this can be a reality.

Someone once told me a helpful way to think about our spiritual rebirth: can we see, hear, touch, taste, or smell when we are saved and born again? Of course not. If we could, so many wouldn't question their salvation over and over. Still, there is something that happens to our spirits once we have been redeemed. Remember when Jesus told Nicodemus he needed to be born again (John 3:1-15)? He meant that Nicodemus' spirit—the part of him that was eternal—would be born again. His spirit would go through a new birth; it would die and be reborn with a fresh covering, washed clean in the blood of Jesus. Just as Paul says in his letter to the Corinthians, "The old has passed away; behold, the new has come" (2 Corinthians 5:17). When we are born in the physical realm, we enter the world as babies—we have new life. The same is true when we are reborn in the spirit—we have new life. This is why Paul tells the Corinthians he fed them with milk instead of solid food because they were still infants in the spirit. Our minds, hearts, and bodies are still in the flesh and fall into the trap of fleshly desires, but our spirits have been made alive and new! This is important to understand in order to see the full picture of what the writers of the New Testament are often speaking of regarding our spirits being reborn.

When we are born again, our spirits are automatically made new and seated in heavenly places. The table is prepared before us as the psalmist speaks about in Psalm 23, is a table within the heavens, with King Jesus and God the Father. Their glory fills the table, and we have the privilege and the right to be seated there.

Even though we are seated in heavenly places, there are times where we can let ourselves get pulled down by the distractions the enemy and this earth throw at us underneath the table. These distractions convince us to take our eyes off the Father and focus on what is going on all around us. The Bible tells us to "seek the things above where Christ is seated at the right hand of God," and "to set our minds on things above" (Colossians 3:1-2). It shows us we have to lift up our eyes while we are seated at the table and look into our Father's eyes. Looking underneath the table is keeping our eyes on the distractions, earthly passions, lusts of this world, our fleshly desires, the chaos and confusion that swirl all around us, the threats of the enemy. Although in the natural realm these things can seem all-consuming and scary, we are still called to set our eyes on the things above. Instead of focusing on the chaos around us, we need to ask the Holy Spirit to give us eyes to see what He is doing in the midst of it all. We must train ourselves through the renewing of our minds to keep our eyes on Him and His work.

No soldier gets entangled in civilian pursuits, since his aim is to please the one who enlisted him.

2 Timothy 2:4

We have to remember we are also seated in the spiritual realm. We must remember our battle is not against flesh and blood, this party or that party, our neighbors, husbands, or kids; it is against something more than what we can see with our natural eyes.

For we do not wrestle against flesh and blood, but against the rulers, against the authorities, against the cosmic powers over this present darkness, against the spiritual forces of evil in the heavenly places.

Ephesians 6:12

Knowing that we have a seat at the table is a big deal because it is where the presence of His glory resides, and where His glory resides there is peace. We have peace knowing we are with the Father and His plans are good. From this place of peace, we can then entrust everything in our lives to our loving Father—

our health, kids, marriages, decisions, and anything else we might face. When I'm at the table and my eyes are on Him, His peace radiates, so my focus is not on the noise underneath. When I'm not at peace, I know I'm distracted and not sitting where I'm supposed to be. Facing the problems underneath the table without first fixing our gaze on Him is like going off to fight an unnecessary battle, and without armor.

Walking in Authority

I have mentioned the authority we carry as sons and daughters of God, but we *need* to understand what this is and how to walk in it. As I think about our authority, I just love how it is touched and given by each member of the Trinity. We have authority as children of the Father who is the King of Kings, we carry authority as temples of the Holy Spirit and vessels of His power and wisdom, and we walk in authority according to the example and mandate of Jesus.

We have authority from the Father because we share in the same inheritance as Jesus. He is the firstborn, so He has been given the greater authority, but we are still children in God's house. Just as a child holds a level of "authority" in her household that a stranger does not hold (i.e. access, favor, decision-making ability for some aspects of the household), so do we in the kingdom of God. No matter the age or maturity of the child, she has free access to the rooms, possessions, and members of the house. No matter how she behaves, she is shown favor, acceptance, and love that a stranger would not be shown by the members of the household. And there are certain areas or possessions of the household that are her "jurisdiction," be they her room, her toys, etc. We must stop walking around like orphans when God calls us sons and daughters. Not accepting our place in God's house and the blessings, rights, and inheritance that come with it is like an adopted child sleeping on the porch and begging for food, refusing to live as a loved and accepted daughter.

We also carry authority because we carry the Holy Spirit. We are vessels to be used for His purposes. If we are living lives surrendered to Him, speaking His words, obeying His leading, and walking in His ways, He will shine out of us more and more. His wisdom, His power, His love, His authority, and all His other attributes will come out of us. Just as Peter commanded the lame man in the temple to stand up and walk (through the power of the Holy Spirit), we also have authority given and walked out by the Holy Spirit in us.

Lastly, we have authority because of the example and command of Jesus Christ. The Bible says Jesus was given all authority in Heaven and earth (Matthew 28:18). We see right after Jesus declared these words He then turned to His disciples and gives them the command to go and make disciples of all nations, "baptizing them in the name of the Father, Son, and Holy Spirit, and teaching them to observe and do all that [He] had commanded [them] to do" (Matthew 28:19-20).

Now, many of us who grew up in the church are very familiar with this passage, also known as the Great Commission. We know we have been called to make disciples and to baptize them, but often, we overlook the fact we have also been called to *teach* them to do what Jesus commanded His disciples to do. If we look back throughout the gospels, we see Jesus gave His disciples authority and commanded them to do specific things; especially when he sent them out two by two. The disciples were commanded to heal the sick, cast out demons, raise the dead, and cleanse the lepers—not just once but multiple times (Matthew 10:1,7-8; Luke 9:1-3). Jesus also went on to tell them authority had been given to them to trample serpents and scorpions and power over the enemy (Luke 10:19). Romans 13:1, also confirms "there is no authority except from God" himself.

Let me be very clear here, this is not our own authority but the authority of the one we have placed our faith in Christ Jesus. And it is not by our own power we can heal the sick, cast out demons, raise the dead, or have victory over the enemy, but only through the power of the Holy Spirit. We see, throughout the epistles, the disciples and Christ-followers of the early church walked in this authority and were well aware of it, yet today, many of us shy away from these beliefs. If we follow and believe the Great Commission, we should also believe and obey that we have been commanded to walk as disciples of Christ and do all that He taught.

Jesus told His disciples, "I tell you this timeless truth: The person who follows me in faith, believing in me, will do the same mighty miracles that I do—even greater miracles than these because I go to be with the Father" (John 14:12, TPT). We are not only called to do the things He did, but He says we will do even greater things. We carry the light of Jesus. It radiates through us. If we are image-bearers, should not all of our actions point back to Him? If Jesus healed the sick, why are we so ashamed to believe He still does? This is the authority you and I have been given, not because of anything we have done, but because of the blood of Jesus. Do not let the enemy make you think you do not carry authority because I can tell you when you start to believe that you carry authority as a son or daughter, you will begin to see things you didn't believe were possible. We carry *power* in the name of Jesus. Do *not* let the enemy take that from you and keep you trapped into thinking that you do not. It is part of who you are, and it is part of your calling to go into the world to make disciples, baptize them, and teach them the power they carry because of who they are in Christ!

Called to Shine

Isaiah 60:1-2 tells us to "rise, shine, for your light has come and the glory of the Lord has risen upon you. For behold, darkness shall cover the earth, and thick darkness the peoples; but the Lord will arise upon you, and His glory will be seen upon you." I want you to understand the power you carry as a disciple and follower of Christ. The Bible is very clear that the darkness is coming and will cover the earth. I believe, in many ways, we are in this very time of darkness. It covers our communities, cities, states, and nations, yet, there is hope. Why? Because we carry the light. We disciples are called to rise and shine, for the Light of God is in us and on us. We carry His glory, and we carry the power of the Holy Spirit within us. As we begin to walk as light-bearers, we get to walk into the darkness and light it up. Scripture says, "And nations shall come to your light, and kings to the brightness of your rising" (Isaiah 60:3). It is through the sons and daughters of God that the light brightens up the darkness.

Many of us are waiting for the Lord to come and move us away from the darkness, but that is not what we have been called to. For we have been created for this time, and we are called to be the ones who shine in the darkness. We bring the light to our neighborhoods, our schools, and our communities. It is His light through us and His truth that brings hope to the hopeless. It is His Spirit of love that shows love to those who feel unlovable. You, my dear brothers and sisters, carry the glory of your Father. This is your purpose. This is your calling: to bring light into the darkness. You don't need to be a Bible scholar or have a theology degree. Jesus touched everyone who had ears to hear, and those seeds grew into flourishing trees that bore fruit, giving food to those around them, as we see at work in the early church of Acts. Oh, the beauty of walking with Him and following Him. Because He loves me so much, I get to be the one that carries His love to those around me. We are His hands and feet—this is how we get to walk!

Declaration (replace my name with yours):

I am Lindsey. I am a daughter of the King. I am loved by Him. No one and nothing can take that away from me. God, my Father, sees me as righteous and holy and above reproach. Because of the blood of Jesus I have been redeemed and forgiven. Even though I did nothing to deserve it, God loved me so much He sent Jesus to take my place. He knows me by name, and He has a seat at the table for me.

$\int i x$

How to Walk with Him

A huge part of learning who we are is learning to walk in the presence of the One who created us. Our identity is found in Him. So, in order to understand who we are, we must *know* Him. As we grow in relationship with and intimate knowledge of Him, we will understand more and more who we are. It's like a beautiful spiral upward. He speaks over us about our true identity as we commune with Him, and we long to go deeper with Him the more we understand who we really are.

Religion or Relationship?

Many of us grew up in religion, dedicated to Sunday morning traditions, Sunday and Wednesday evenings filled with potluck meals, AWANAS, and Sunday school meetings, yet we still didn't feel any closer to God. Why is that? Because we were not called to walk in religion. Religion is defined by the Merriam-Webster dictionary as a "personal set or institutionalized system of religious attitudes, beliefs, and practices."[9] What if we shifted from thinking about following God as a religion to actually having a relationship with Him? We have been called to a relationship with God; however, we have made Him into a religion—a system of beliefs, practices, attitudes, programs, institutionalized times to meet and worship. If we are honest, most of us walk in and out of the church building on Sundays and then give God very little thought throughout the week. We might try to keep up the practices we were taught, doing our best to have the right attitudes, beliefs, and habits, so it is frustrating when we fail over and over again. Many of us get stuck, knowing we are saved by grace, but we're still striving to earn our salvation through work because our head-knowledge of grace hasn't actually felt like our experience.

Good news! God is not a religion. Praise Jesus for that. You see, all He has ever asked of us is that we come into relationship with Him. Since the Garden of Eden, we have been called into an intimate relationship with Abba. Just as Adam and Eve walked the garden with the Father, Son, and Holy Spirit, we are invited to do the same. We have the opportunity to walk with God through every moment in our lives. Yes, the fall has made that hard, but we have been given a perfect example in Jesus, who walked perfectly in relationship with His Father. I'm not saying we will always walk perfectly, but I believe if we accept the invitation to walk in relationship with Him in our everyday lives, we will see the old, religious ways of doing things fall off and the ways of the Kingdom of God begin to be established within us.

Walking in Relationship with God

Walking in a relationship involves pursuing someone else. When we start to pursue a relationship with God, we need to recognize He is not just some genie in the sky but He is a real Father who wants to communicate with us and be with us. A relationship changes the dynamic because it allows us to see Him as real, visceral, and conversational-one who actually cares and wants to be in a relationship with us.

In Song of Solomon 1:15, the King speaks to his lover, "Behold, you are beautiful, my love; behold, you are beautiful; your eyes are doves." I remember reading *The Sacred Journey*[10] by Brian and Candice Simmons and truly seeing God is relentlessly chasing after my affection for Him. I started to see the Song of Solomon verses written to a lover as the things God was speaking and singing over me. It began to shift the way I saw Him because I started seeing Him as someone who is earnestly chasing after me and whose deepest desire is that I would stop and see Him for who He truly is—the Lover and Keeper of my soul. He is and will always be my Savior, but He is also the Bridegroom, the One returning for His beautiful bride whom He loves with an unfathomable love.

I am reminded of *The Lion, The Witch, and the Wardrobe*, when Lucy enters Narnia through the wardrobe. At first, she is startled by what she sees, but the more that she is in Narnia, the more she begins to believe what she is experiencing. She becomes so captivated, she excitedly runs to tell her siblings, and although they don't believe her at first, she knows what she saw was real. A little farther on in the story, Lucy and her siblings began to develop a fondness of Narnia and a close relationship with its inhabitants. I love this story because it is such a beautiful picture of believers operating in the spiritual realm. The more we walk in the Spirit and enter a relationship with the Father, the more we will see the way the heavenly Kingdom operates. This is just like Peter, Susan, Edmund, and Lucy seeing how Narnia operated. They began to learn the truth about Aslan and his kingdom. The more they learned, the closer they grew to Aslan the lion, the true king of Narnia.

A relationship takes time to develop. It doesn't happen overnight, and it often comes about through many subtle advances towards the other person and vice versa. This is what we are being invited into: an intimate relationship with the Father, the Son, and the Holy Spirit. We have the opportunity to step into something more than just a religion, tradition, checklist, or routine. He wants us to come fully into communion with Him.

I can tell you trust takes time to build. My relationship with God has changed dramatically, especially these last several years. For most of my life, I knew in my head everything God says is true, yet I would let my natural circumstances dictate in my mind whether He was good, loving, or trustworthy. I let my emotions rule, and often, if I didn't get what I prayed for, I would feel offended He didn't do what I wanted Him to. I prayed but I usually stayed too busy to stop and listen to Him and spend time with Him. More often than not, He was the last place I would seek help. Sound familiar? If I'm honest, it was a one-way relationship. I had head knowledge from the verses I had memorized, the Bible classes I had taken, and the many Bible studies I had participated in, yet the God I'd heard about so often just seemed so far away. I had no concept of what it was like to walk in a day-to-day relationship with Him or that He still speaks to us today and not just through the Bible.

As you read in my testimony, all of that changed the night I had an encounter with Him. The head knowledge shifted to my heart. He spoke, and everything I had studied and read as a child came bursting through and sprung to life. He was there all along, but I had pushed Him out of the way. I had closed the door on Him time and time again, with excuses that, "I'm too busy," "I'll spend time with Him later," "I'm tired because I worked all day," or "I don't have time because the kids need me." I began to realize I will find time to pursue the things I truly love and God wasn't those things.

Have you ever been there? Wondering how you lost your way? Asking, "How did the things I have put first in my life become the first things?" My hope for you, and for me, is God becomes so real to us that we have no other option than to put Him first. I pray you are made aware of His presence right now and you will feel His pursuit.

I love the story of the prodigal son in Luke 15. I can completely understand the youngest son because I was a prodigal too. I ran off to pursue my own heart's interests, desires, and passions, only to be left hurt and completely let down. I had chased after everything I thought I wanted, but I still felt empty, lacking contentment and happiness. Then, like the prodigal son, I began to realize what I was chasing would never be fulfilling.

It is not just the son that draws me to the story. It's also the father. The father waited day after day, looking for his son to come home. But the part where I get weak in the knees and emotional is when the father began to run to his son. This is important because Jewish men of this culture, especially men of wealth, did not run. It would have been considered disgraceful and deeply frowned upon. He most likely would have had to run through the city walls, or the town gates to get to his son, passing many who were highly respected. Yet, this father ran to his son! He humbled and exposed himself, pulling his tunic above his knees, and he ran to embrace a son who had dishonored and disgraced him. He left all of the opinions of others behind him and went against societal norms to get to his son. This shows he was unashamed of his child and all he cared about was that his son had come home. I believe he also knew his son was probably the talk of the town. He had gone and squandered his dad's money. Still, the father picked up his clothes and RAN to his son.

The parable doesn't end there either. Not only did the father run to his son, he threw him a party to celebrate his return!

This parable was told by Jesus to paint us a picture of what it is like to be a child of God. He was showing us there is more to the Father than just existing as this supernatural being and He really is a Father full of love for us, even when we are at our worst. This story is a beautiful picture of how God runs to each one of us. He runs to us, unashamed of where we have been or what we have done; then, Abba celebrates that we have come home. As Zephaniah 3:17, says, "He will rejoice over you with gladness; He will quiet you by his love; He will exult over you with loud singing."

The more we believe in and experience God's pursuit of us, the more hungry we will be for a relationship with Him. There is something about Him that draws you closer the more you see of Him. It's hard to put into words. It's like an intoxication, not from a substance or alcohol, but a holy intoxication, being in the presence of the One who spoke life into your very being.

Intimacy and Communication wth God

Communion—what is it? Communion is defined as the sharing and exchanging of intimate thoughts and feelings, especially when the exchange is on a mental and/or spiritual level.[11] It is learning to walk deeper in the things He wants and thinks; an exchanging of wants and needs for His. Just as the priests of the Old Testament cared for the needs of the people, we, as priests of the Most High, are called to walk with Him and minister to His heart. It is not because He needs anyone to minster to Him, but He longs for this from His children. It is a sacred and intimate exchange of coming into His glory with an open posture, not in need of anything, but just seeking to be in His presence to sit with Him.

At times, this looks like me lying on the floor, face down posture, just wanting to lie at His feet. There are times when His glory enters the room and being in His presence and knowing He is my Creator causes me to weep. This intimacy has come during times of worship at church, where He enters the sanctuary, and all I can do is fall on my knees in awe of His love for me. I have felt it in the quiet place, when I'm sitting with Him and telling Him what is on my heart or while reading His Word. I can remember one particular time when I knew I just needed to be in His presence after a long day with the kids. I had heavy burdens on my heart. I sat listening to worship music and just laying down at His feet what was on my heart. I was envisioning myself literally picking up bags and laying them down at the foot of the cross, when I felt an overwhelming sense overtake me. I saw in the spirit as He knelt down beside me and began to wipe my tears off my cheeks. He just sat there comforting me and letting me know He was very present.

How do we move towards a more intimate relationship with God, learning to walk in communion with Him? A relationship is a connection to someone, while an intimate relationship is defined as "an interpersonal relationship that involves physical and emotional connection."[12] I began to search deeper into what defines an intimate relationship. In one article I read, a psychologist stated that seven elements define what it means to have an intimate relationship. The first element is feeling safe to share knowledge and personal information about everything from our dreams to the things we struggle with. The second is interdependence on the other person. This means influencing them in everyday decisions, such as the food they eat or where they live, to what they do for entertainment, etc. The rest of the elements of an intimate relationship were care, trust, responsiveness to the other's needs, mutually seeing one another as interconnected, and commitment to one another. While this is a secular definition of intimacy, I believe we can use it to get a glimpse into what it looks like to walk in intimacy with the Father.

Walking in intimacy with God is a difficult thing to articulate. In my life, I have found intimacy with Him starts with conversation. It's simply a conversation where you sit and share your heart. He sees it all anyway, so why do we feel the need to hide it or tuck it down? He is wanting to fully restore us from our innermost thoughts, our deepest pains, and things we put away in the closet of our minds. He sees it all and knows it all. His Word says nothing is hidden from His sight (Psalm 38:9), He hears every thought before we even utter it out of our mouth (Psalm 139:4), and He sees every deed (Psalm 69:5). Intimacy is sitting at his feet and telling Him everything, holding nothing back because He is not ashamed of us and is not judging us. Instead, He holds us, comforts us, and then, as only a loving Father could, He speaks into our pain and confusion and answers our questions.

When He speaks, His words are always full of life and truth. He speaks life into the very places of our hearts and lives that are broken. We often cling so tightly to things that happened in the past. He has asked me to lay these things down in order to get rid of what was causing toxicity and pain within me. It reminds me that we are told in Hebrews 12:1-2, to, "lay aside every weight, and sin which clings so closely, and let us run with endurance the race that is set before us, looking to Jesus..." or in Isaiah 43:18-19, where the Lord says, "Remember not the former things, nor consider the things of old. Behold, I am doing a new thing; now it springs forth, do you not perceive it? I will make a way in the wilderness and rivers in the desert." It hurts at the moment to put down things I have been holding onto, but looking back, I see it has left space for Him to come in and make me whole. That's just one of the privileges of walking in intimacy with Him.

As the conversation grows with Him, we begin to see the way He is subtly speaking to us in our everyday lives and routines. It is a dialogue that continues throughout the day, from the time we wake up to the time our head hits the pillow at night. Even then, I have often experienced God is still speaking to me even as I sleep. He knows exactly when to speak to us, and learning to listen becomes part of walking with Him. People will often hear me say walking with the Father is like a never-ending treasure hunt because, when you say yes to Him and have a posture of listening, every day is a new conversation and a new adventure. Having an intimate relationship with the Father requires mutual commitment. He has already committed to us 100% and is waiting on us to give Him the same commitment. He's offering us companionship and waiting for us to step into it.

When I think of intimacy with the Father, I think of Mary, in John 12:3-5, pouring out her alabaster jar of expensive oil on Jesus' feet. To anoint Jesus, she gave the most valuable thing she had. She sat at His feet, wiping them with her hair. This is such an intimate moment, and she did this as the disciples and others in the room watched. She was criticized for her actions, but she didn't care. She continued pouring the oil out and wiping His feet with her hair. Are we willing to pour out everything we have and sit at His feet? Are we so in love with Jesus that nothing can distract us?

As with any relationship, when we start to spend more time with a person, we come to know their likes and dislikes. 1 John 1:6 hints at this: "If we say we have fellowship with Him while we walk in darkness, we lie and do not practice the truth." The more we walk in intimate fellowship and relationship, the more aware we become of things that are pleasing and displeasing to Him. We will also find our desire for God grows stronger. For example, I know my husband's likes and dislikes. The more intimate he and I become, the more I want to do what I know he likes. I do it out of love, not obligation, because I have spent time with him and let my affections for him grow. Therefore, walking in darkness would be clear evidence that we're not truly intimate with God. Our relationship with God, or lack thereof, will always begin to spill out into everyday life, becoming evident to those around us. The more intimately we walk with the Father, the more our lives will bear the fruits of His Spirit: love, joy, peace, patience, kindness, goodness, faithfulness, gentleness, and self-control (Galatians 5:22). These will begin to flow out into the relationships around us, as we spend more time with Him.

It is important to point out we cannot compare our relationship and intimacy with God to someone else's. Each of us has a unique relationship with Him. Isn't that the beauty of any relationship or friendship? It is also important to recognize Jesus had twelve disciples, but only a few of them were intimate and close with him. I believe this is because Peter, James, and John pursued Him; they desired more of Him. They were not afraid to get close, diving deep into conversations with Him, even if they spoke out of line like we see Peter often do. It is these three who shared intimate time with Jesus just moments before He went to the cross: from the upper room where they had the Lord's supper to the garden of Gethsemane. Jesus brought them farther into the garden than the other disciples, and He opened up and told them, "My soul is very sorrowful, even to death" (Matthew 26:38). He instructed them to stay awake and watch. This shows another dynamic of the relationship, in which He spoke what was on His heart to closest friends rather than to all of them. Intimacy with Him involves having an open posture of receiving but also availability. It's a reciprocal relationship.

Walking in a relationship with God has been a continual journey and adventure for me. It's a heart posture of not just receiving but of sitting at His feet praising Him and giving Him thanks. It's knowing He loves me, that He calls me His daughter, that He is unashamed of me, and that I'm beautiful-the apple of His eye. I know these things because He whispers them to me gently in the moments I need to hear them most.

It's when I imagine the look in His eyes, when He lifts up my head and says, "I know your heart is heavy, daughter, but I'm here. Come sit with me and let me hold you." I have been held by Him in the darkest of hours—in those early mornings when I have expressed to Him everything is sinking and I just can't seem to see past my circumstances. Intimacy grows as I understand His heart for humanity. Intimacy is learning to cry out for what is on His heart and to intercede and lift up prayers back to Him. It is those moments I treasure the most.

I believe intimacy and relationship are what He is calling us to at this time, but we have become so distracted by the noise of this world we haven't heard Him. We haven't made time for God; He has just become a comfortable add-on to our lives because we grew up Christian or because it feels easy to follow the status quo of those around us who call themselves Christians. Or, maybe we just haven't known what it actually looks like to walk in an intimate relationship with Him. I know many of us have lost our way in what it really means to walk in communion with God, but I'm here to tell you it's not too late. The Father longs for intimacy with His children and is giving us an open invitation. Why would we not accept and jump headfirst into a relationship with Love Himself?

Seven

Repent and Renew

So far, we have discussed who the Father, Jesus, and the Holy Spirit are, and who we are as children of God. We have talked about how to walk in intimacy and communion with God, and what it looks like to carry out a relationship with Him as sons and daughters. I want us to look at how we can align our hearts and minds with the Father's and what actions we are to take from there.

Repentance

From that time Jesus began to preach, saying,
"Repent, for the kingdom of Heaven is at hand."

Matthew 4:17

"Repent" here is the Greek word "metanoeō,"[14] which means "to change the way you think." Repentance is the call for us to literally do a 180-degree turn in our thinking. It is changing the way we think about everything and learning to view things with a kingdom perspective.

The Bible tells us John the Baptist paved the way for Jesus, calling the people to repent, to change the way they thought and lived because the kingdom of God was at hand (Matthew 3:2). You see, Jesus came into the world to redeem God's children and be the sacrifice that would set us free from the law. Every sin, every wrong decision, every thought, every action, everything not of God we have done, Jesus already bore on the cross. We have been forgiven for it all, but we must take action. We have been called to repent, to come to His feet and lay down all of our ways, thoughts, and actions, and to surrender completely to Him.

The beauty of repentance is we are called to come as we are. He takes us as we are, no matter how filthy. I love how The Passion Translation words Colossian 3:3-4: "Your crucifixion with Christ has severed the tie to this life, and now your true life is hidden away in God in Christ. And as Christ Himself is seen for who He really is, who you really are will also be revealed, for you are now one with Him in His glory!" In the next several verses, Paul continues on to say that we must put to death anything earthly in us, putting off the old self with its practices and putting on the new self (Colossians 3:5-10). Since God takes us just as we are, there is nothing we need to fix before we come into His presence.

I have heard people say, "Well, I need to do this and this before I come to Him," but that's not what God says. We see throughout the Word of God He takes us just the way we are: broken, addicted, scared, unsure, rebellious, a prodigal, etc. He says come as you are, and His arms are wide open. This is the thing that so often brings me to my knees in awe and love for Him. Why? Because I know all I carried and laid down at His feet. I came broken, a prodigal who had run away from Him, foolishly thinking I could find pleasure elsewhere. I came with my problems, with my rebel heart, and laid them down saying, "I want you and only you." This is the beauty of the love God has for each of us! Jesus Himself said, "Who goes to the doctor for a cure? Those who are well or those who are sick? I have not come to call the 'righteous,' but to call those who are sinners and bring them to repentance" (Mark 2:17, TPT). Jesus came to bring the "sick and sinners," the outcasts and the ones His society saw and rejected, to Himself and to the Father. As we repent and bring our sin to Jesus, calling out He is the true King and we are not, we then begin to walk as transformed spirits. This doesn't mean everything we struggled with falls off right away; although, I have seen the Spirit of God completely remove addictions from people as they fall at His feet. Most of the time, it is a surrender to the Spirit to come in and begin to cultivate new roots and soil that bear fruit.

So what does repentance look like? It starts with us confessing Jesus is the Son of God. Feel free to use the sample prayer below as a guide, but then make it your own. Be yourself, go to him as you are, and ask Him to speak to you.

"Jesus, I believe you died for my sins, you alone are my Savior, and God is the One True God. I come before you confessing my need for you. I give you my life. I am turning away from living for myself, and I'm going to follow you. Lead me in your ways."

If you just prayed this as a personal prayer, I would encourage you to tell another believer so you can get encouragement and discipleship. We are told in Hebrews 10:25, not to neglect meeting together as believers, and Scripture tells us we are the body of Christ, each having been given gifts we're meant to serve the body with, so it's important we are in a community of true believers. If you don't have someone to tell or get connected with, feel free to reach out to me (you can find my email in the bio at the end of this book), and I would love to welcome you to the family and point you to some action steps that could be helpful as you begin your new journey of following Jesus.

For those reading this who have confessed Jesus as Lord and have given their lives to Him, repentance now looks like a daily taking up of our cross and following Him. It is a moment-by-moment lifestyle of taking every thought captive to the obedience of Christ and fighting off temptation right away with the truth of God's Word. It is a turning from our sin, not just outwardly but inwardly, actively, intentionally, and consistently so we are no longer living like we're still slaves to sin. When we practice repentance, we get farther and farther from the chains that have already been broken off of us, and we become more and more like who he made us to be - being conformed to the image of Christ, living in holiness and freedom

Renewing our Minds

Do not be conformed to this world, but be transformed by the renewal of your mind, that by testing you may discern what is the will of God, what is good and acceptable and perfect.

Romans 12:2

...and to be renewed in the spirit of your minds...

Ephesians 4:23

What does Paul mean when he talks about renewing your mind? The Greek word for the phrase "renewing your mind" is "anakainōsis."[15] It means "to renovate and completely change for the better." Thankfully, we have been given help with this. We have the perfect Helper at our disposal. Jesus promised us a Helper in John 15:26: "But when the Helper comes, whom I will send to you from the Father, the Spirit of truth, who proceeds from the Father, He will bear witness about me."

To renew our minds means to allow the Holy Spirit to transform the way we think and, therefore, act. It is the clearing out of the old and the bringing in of the new. It doesn't always happen overnight but is often a gradual change into becoming more like Christ. It is the process of dying to self and learning my wants, my control, the way I thought things should be, and all the false truths I have believed through the years have to be crucified. It is fully surrendering our lives into the Father's hands and allowing Him to search our hearts and expose lies and false theologies.

He who has clean hands and a pure heart, who does not lift up his soul to what is false...He will receive blessing from the Lord and righteousness from the God of his salvation.

Psalm 24:4-5

Search me, O God, and know my heart! Try me and know my thoughts! And see if there be any grievous way in me, and lead me in the way of everlasting!

Psalm 139:23-24

To renew our minds is to focus on the things of the Spirit. It is the training of one's mind to stop it from thinking on the things of the flesh and to change its course to focus on what the kingdom says. Scripture says we've been made new in Christ's likeness when we come to place our faith in Him. We see this in 2 Corinthians 5:17: "Therefore, if anyone is in Christ, he is a new creation. The old has passed away; behold, the new has come." In 2 Corinthians 4:16, it says, "So we do not lose heart. Though our outer self is wasting away, our inner self is being renewed day by day." These verses are stating we have been given a new spirit, one that is completely transformed into the likeness of Christ. We still have our flesh, minds, and emotions that struggle with earthly ways. It is this body and flesh that is wasting away, but our spirit is what will live on forever. When we accept Jesus as Lord, our spirit is reborn and made anew by the blood of Jesus; it is completely transformed.

We are told in Colossians 3:1-2, to seek the things that are above, where Christ is seated at the right hand of God. How do we align our mind and body to think in line with our spirit? We start focusing on what is true, allowing the Holy Spirit to come in and start to prune and cut away the things that are not in agreement with what God says. Now, this process is not always pretty. Trust me; it is often quite painful. Any perspective we have that does not agree with Heaven's truth has to go. The more married we are to our own perspective, the more painful but necessary this process is.

One example from my own life is my struggle with body image. For the last few years, the Lord has been chopping off the bad roots and branches and aligning my mindset with what He says about me. It looks kind of like this: I will stare in the mirror and think thoughts of, "I'm so ugly and overweight," but then, that little tug within starts to replay verses of truth. Now when

I start doing this, I have begun to catch myself and say, "No; that is not true. I am beautifully and wonderfully created in the image of God. I am beloved and chosen by God. I am seated in heavenly places in an eternal throne room that has no end. My flesh is passing away, but Lord, you have given me a spirit that lives on forever with you." It is a process of learning to stop our flesh and mind from thinking about the things of this world and what the enemy is whispering to us.

We must shift our perspectives and think about the things of the Spirit and the truth of God's Word. As you begin to do this, something begins to shift inside. I can't explain it, but it's like you become more bold and confident, and that mindset you struggled with starts to fall away, and the new one starts to take root. Author and cognitive neuroscientist, Dr. Caroline Leaf, talks about how our brains actually regrow new pathways as we actively choose to think differently. Brain scans have actually picked up the differences in neural pathways and show that by changing the way we think and speak over ourselves, we can literally rewire our brains.[16] This helps us to understand the renewing and guarding of our thoughts makes an impact on us.

It is so important for us to keep a close guard on our thoughts. We know that one of the enemy's favorite tactics is to twist truth and cause confusion in our minds so we spiral mentally and emotionally. The little lies we believe can so easily turn into stubborn mindsets or harmful misconceptions. Pastor Chad Norris, of Bridgeway Church, says often in his sermons and his "Coach & Joe" podcast, that a misconception is a very dangerous thing. We must constantly be renewing our minds and setting our minds on the things above. Our thoughts must align with what the Father's heart is for a situation. In order to do this, we must know the truth found in His Word. If we don't know the truth, we leave ourselves susceptible to being misled into believing a lie.

Something I see often is a parent, friend, or classmate will speak negative words over a child, and the child begins to believe those words and even say them to themselves. "I'm fat. I'm slow. I'm not good enough..." These words are like seeds that begin to take root in our minds and make themselves comfortable, so much so they become what we think and believe about ourselves. I have learned when it comes to renewing our minds, a great place to start is by asking the Lord to reveal lies and to expose the truth. In Psalm 25:4-5 (NASB), we read a request to the Lord from the psalmist asking Him for these things, "Make me know your ways, O Lord; teach me your paths. Lead me in your truth and teach me, for you are the God of my salvation; for you I wait all the day." This is the posture we should take when we start to ask the Holy Spirit to reveal within us things that do not line up with what He says is true. Once He reveals the lie we're believing, we must then start speaking truth over it and let the truth rewire the way our minds think about that thing.

For example, if someone had spoken over you that you were not smart enough to do something, that lie might penetrate to the point that it starts to take residence without you knowing it. When you go to do something the person said you weren't smart enough to do, that memory pops up, perhaps even subconsciously, and tells your mind you can't do that because you just aren't smart enough to do it. What has happened is that the lie has become true to you and is now stopping you from doing what you really are smart enough to do. One way to renew your mind is by repenting for coming into agreement with that word, then rebuking it.

Here's what I mean:

"Father, I confess to believing you created me as anything other than good, as your Word says in Genesis. I rebuke the words spoken over me, that I'm not smart enough to do (insert lie here). I renounce coming into agreement with it and confess I have not believed you for what you said about me. For you created me in your image; you created me for a purpose; I am smart enough to do whatever you have placed inside of me to do. You created me for your glory. You had a plan for me since the beginning of time, and you knew exactly how I needed to be knitted together in order to carry out what you spoke over me. Holy Spirit, I pray you would help me to trust what the Father has said about me, and I declare today I am smart enough, and I was created exactly how I should have been created. In Jesus' name, I pray, amen."

This is what I started doing as the Holy Spirit started asking me, "Who told you that?" and revealing things spoken about me that I had started to believe as true. As we begin to renew our minds, we come to truly understand who our Heavenly Father is and our identity in Him. This happens as He reveals mindsets that are not from Him and as we set our minds on heavenly things. I can't encourage you enough to re-read the above, and I pray that He gives you a clear revelation of who you are.

My prayer for you:

Oh, Father! Thank you for your love for us. Thank you for sending your only Son to take our place on the cross, to cover us in a blanket of righteousness. We thank you for who you say we are if we have faith. We are holy, righteous, beloved, royal, daughters, and sons of the highest King, whose kingdom knows no end. We have an everlasting inheritance in you. We are rejoiced over. We are seen by the One who created all things. Thank you! Today, we come asking you to open our eyes to the work you have already done for us, to the works you have already claimed victory over at the cross. I pray those who read this book would have their eyes open to the tactics of the evil one; that their eyes will be locked in on you and your love for them. Holy Spirit, we expose the lies for what they are and ask you to battle on our behalf. We pray you would speak truth over us, that we tune out the voice of the evil one and only hear the truth that leaves your lips. Give us a clear revelation of our true identity. Let us be daughters and sons who only feast at your table and show your love! In Jesus' name, we pray, Amen.

Eight

Our Purpose as Daughters and Sons

"Why was I created? What is my purpose here on earth?" These are questions all of us ponder at some point. The question of our purpose is a good one, and it is one worth getting an answer to.

How Were We Created?

Before we can answer the question of *why* we were created, I believe we need to look at *how* we were created:

> *Then God said, "Let us make man in our image, after our likeness. And let them have dominion over the fish of the sea and over the birds of the heavens and over the livestock and over all the earth and over every creeping thing that creeps on the earth." So God created man in his own image, in the image of God He created them; male and female He created them.*
>
> Genesis 1:26-27

There is no other earthly creature or angelic being like us because we are created to resemble God Himself. Just like children resemble their biological parents in the natural world, we were created to resemble our Heavenly Father. In the passage above, I want us to notice two things. First, the words "Let us." God is speaking in plural form, meaning that the Trinity—God the Father, God the Son, and God the Holy Spirit—is at work together in the creation of the Earth. We are created in the image of all *three* persons of the Trinity. I think it is extremely important to notice this. Why? Because I believe each person of the Trinity carries their own individual traits, as I discussed in the first few chapters of this book. Each person of the Trinity is different, yet together, they are fully *one God*. This is just one of the wonders and beauties of our Creator. It is one of the mysteries of God to search out as He reveals more of Himself to those who walk in intimacy with Him.

The second thing to notice in this passage is we are all human beings created in God's own image, both men and women. How can men and women both be made in the image of God? I believe God carries both masculine and feminine traits. We know He has qualities that are more often seen as masculine, such as His might and strength, His role as protector, defender, provider, etc. He also has beautiful characteristics that are typically seen as feminine. Some of these attributes that first come to mind are His nurturing and comforting nature. He cares for every one of His children's needs. This makes me think of a mother kissing her child's scraped knee or nursing her crying infant. I have seen this maternal nature in how God jealously fights for His kids and longs for them to come home.

My maternal instincts, which are so innate, powerful, and important for the wellbeing of my children; I didn't create them in myself, and they're not just random. They point to such a specific design by an Almighty Creator. They point to His maternal nature. There's no way I can be more nurturing, caring, or protective than the God whose image I reflect. God is described in Deuteronomy 32:10-12, as caring, like a mothering eagle that "flutters over its young, spreading out its wings, catching them, bearing them on its pinions..." And in Matthew 23:37, Jesus says He would have gathered Jerusalem "as a hen gathers her brood under her wings." I love these glimpses in Scripture of His maternal nature. Reverend Naus of Moody Church writes in an article on this topic that "when we think of God's love for those who are reconciled to him in Jesus, we not only think of a strong, protective and wise father, but we can also bask in his tender, nurturing, comforting care seen most beautifully in a mother's love for her child" (Naus 2011).[17] He gives the example of how God can be like a mama bear, whose wrath becomes kindled when her kids are criticized and provoked.[18] In his book *Fashioned to Reign*, Kris Valloton writes: "It takes both women and men to accurately represent the Godhead, as we were both created in the image of God. God is not human, but neither is God a male. It takes both feminine and masculine characteristics to represent God to the world."[19] I love this reminder that God carries both female and male attributes, and in order to fully walk as image-bearers of Him, we must understand both men and women are created in His image.

Never have we been so confused over identity in the church and culture as a whole as we are today. I believe the confusion is that we don't know who we are as sons and daughters of God, and we don't know the authority we carry. Our society says that gender is fluid and doesn't necessarily depend on the body parts we were born with. It says we can and must decide for *ourselves* what gender we are. As sons and daughters of God, we can't let culture or our own fleshly desires dictate who God says we are. This has left so many of us in a crippling identity crisis. Instead, we must listen to His voice and allow His kingdom to influence us.

Another massive area in which our identity is being attacked is in how our culture views men and women in terms of roles and equality. What began as a fight against injustice towards women has turned into an attack on both masculinity and femininity. Incredible, God-given callings like motherhood are being belittled. Men, who were created to lead, protect, and provide are being told now to take a backseat. The enemy has had a field day with God's original design for family and society and has wreaked such havoc that now it is easy to view God's original design as oppressive or narrow-minded. But could it be that the issue was never with God's design, but instead with our false understanding of our identity?

Kris Vallotton often says, "We are the first fatherless generation where our fathers have not gone off to war." Why is this? One of the reasons is the attack on the identity of the man. Instead of being strengthened and built up in courage and servant-leadership, men are being told they are unintelligent, inadequate, and unnecessary; they are being encouraged to exchange their masculinity for femininity. And yet, we read in Scripture it is the men who are called to represent Jesus as the heads of their households through Christ-like love and leadership. They have been created by God for a place of honor and hard work.

But this doesn't have any implications on the worth of women.

Throughout Scripture, we see Jesus honoring women and treating them with respect and acknowledgment of their worth and significance. He defends them, speaks to them like equals, blesses them, and comes to them first both in His birth and resurrection. In no part of God's design are women considered *less*-than. We can tend to have skewed perspectives on this, often because of the biblical call for wives to submit to their husbands, but we forget Jesus submitted in *all* things to the Father. Did that make him less-than? If we really understood who God made us to be and how He views us, we would no longer feel the need to fight and prove ourselves or put others down, belittling their God-given callings and roles.

These are just some of the areas we have become wrapped up in, leaving this generation questioning identity and purpose like never before. Before repairing anything, it is best to first repent, which is changing the way we think. I strongly believe this is the generation that God has set aside to rise up and claim back what belongs to Him. I believe we are the Isaiah 61:4, generation, which says: "They shall build up the ancient ruins; they shall raise up the former devastations; they shall repair the ruined cities, the devastations of many generations." I believe we will become this generation as we step into our true identity. How? By searching for the answer in His Word about who we are and starting to walk in our God-given purpose and authority. As we begin to walk in simple obedience to His Word and what it says, we will then walk unashamed and full of boldness and courage. We lean into Him by sitting at His feet and listening to what He whispers quietly in our spirits. We have been called to be priests, ministering to Him and surrendering to Him out of a pure heart. This is where we will start to see our lives and our generation transform and actually be who He has called us to be.

Why Were We Created?

How many of us have asked this question: Why were we created? As the catechism says, we were created to "glorify God." But, we have also been called to love him, walk with him, and know him.

I believe we see this original intent in Genesis 1-2, where we see Adam and Eve walking with God. They loved him, they knew Him, and they glorified Him through who they were and through living out their God-given purpose with the authority He had given them. We see that this changed the moment they ate of the forbidden tree, and they realized they were naked and became ashamed of who they were. Prior to the fall, they walked with God in an intimate relationship, but after they ate of the tree of good and evil, we are told they heard His footsteps and hid because they were afraid. In one instant, the beauty of walking with Him became shame.

The good part for us is the story doesn't end there. We get to see the other part of the story: redemption. This is where Jesus enters the story generations later and steps onto earth as a man. John 3:16-17, tells us that "God so loved the world that He gave His only Son, that whoever believes in Him should not perish but have eternal life." It goes on, "for God did not send his Son into the world to condemn the world, but in order that the world might be saved through him." God redeemed the story because of His great love for His children. He sent Jesus to be born of a virgin; to enter the world as a man and be the ultimate sacrifice to bring His children back to Him. What amazing love! He gave *everything* in order to rescue His lost children. This is the gospel, the gift of a perfect lamb and the sacrifice needed to bring us back into alignment with our original purpose to glorify God, walk with Him, love Him, and know Him. This is not through sacrifices and rituals but through communion and intimacy with Him.

"For I am the Lord your God, the Holy One of Israel, your Savior. I give Egypt as your ransom, Cush and Seba in exchange for you. Because you are precious in my eyes, and honored, and I love you, I give men in return for you, peoples in exchange for your life. Fear not, for I am with you; I will bring your offspring from the east, and from the west I will gather you. I will say to the north, Give up, and to the south, Do not withhold; bring my sons from afar and my daughters from the end of the earth, everyone who is called by my name, whom I created for my glory, whom I formed and made."

Isaiah 43:3-7

Ultimately, we were created to glorify God in all we say and do. No matter what season we are in, we are called to glorify God. He is the Lord God, the one who chases after us, who loves us, honors us, and will give anything to bring us back to Him. Why would we not want to bring honor and glory to Him for all He has done for us? This is why we were created-to walk with God, to seek Him and know Him, to know His ways, know His heart, and to bring it to those around us. We are to love Him, love others, and love ourselves because that is His heart and command for us. "You shall love the Lord your God with all your heart and with all your soul and with all your mind and with all your strength. The second is this:

'You shall love your neighbor as yourself.' There is no other commandment greater than these" (Mark 12:30-31). We are to glorify Him, in everything we do and say. When we begin to walk in our original intent as sons and daughters, our purpose becomes clear to us.

What is Our Unique Purpose?

We were created to bring God glory and to walk in a relationship with Him, but we were also created uniquely with individual gifts, callings, and good works that He set aside for us to perform before we were even born. Our purpose is to live in light of these things and to walk them out.

As we go on the journey of walking with God, we learn more about the authority we carry on this earth as His sons and daughters. We might not always understand our circumstances, but no matter what season of life we are in, we are called to glorify God. This starts with putting to use what He has given us for each season and thanking and praising Him in the process, regardless of how we feel about the situation. We know that each one of us was created differently. No two of us are the same. So, while we were all created to glorify God, our specific aim and intent will be different from that of our brother or sister in Christ. We were made to flow as one body, and just like our physical bodies, each part has a different role to play, with different abilities and purposes.

God has made me uniquely different from my husband, parents, sons, and friends, and He has done this for a purpose. He has placed dreams, visions, gifts, and talents inside of me that He has called me to walk out and accomplish. My path looks different from anyone else, and that is the mystery of God and the beauty of how each of us has been uniquely made.

While we have all been called to give praise, glory, and thanksgiving to the Lord, there are those who have been given specific talents of music, singing, and songwriting. Their purpose would be to bring God glory and honor through their songs, music, worship, and praise, and maybe even to lead others around them in that as well. Another example is the gift of caring for the sick. We have all been called to "pray for the sick, take care of the sick," but there are those, like doctors and nurses, who God has given talents with their hands and mind to be able to care for and treat the sick. As a nurse, I'm there to bring Him glory, whether through silently praying over the rooms or the hallways in the hospital, being a listening ear to a patient, or being intentional to respond to coworkers in love rather than in judgment or gossip. I have seen the more I do these things, the more He shows me His heart for that day or that person. It then becomes my honor, as His daughter, to carry out and boldly step into the purpose for which He has placed me there at that time. It's one step at a time, one day at a time.

Many of you might claim not to have any talents or gifts, or you may simply belittle them. But God has made you unique and placed His image within you. He made you with a purpose and there is nothing insignificant about what or who He creates. I believe the Lord uses each season of our lives, from childhood and adolescence to adulthood, to train us, teach us, and grow us in a way that points us toward our purpose. In each one of these seasons, we are called to bring Him glory. I can testify that as we start walking in our specific, God-given purposes, we start to see our relationship with Him grow. He delights in seeing His kids be all He made us to be. What parent would not delight in seeing their child use their gifts and thrive in them?

As we walk more with God's purpose for us and those around us in mind, we see more of God's heart for people. We start to realize that we are not just here to simply exist, but that we were created to carry His heart into the earth by actively calling His will down from Heaven. We were created to rule and reign on the earth by bringing our Father's heart to it and speaking life to what is dead and dying around us. Remember, the thief is the one who comes "to steal, kill, and destroy." Jesus came to give life and life abundantly (John 10:10). While this is speaking of eternal life, it also is speaking about the life He brings to the things broken here on earth. Jesus is the perfect role model for that. Everything we saw Him do on earth shows us how to walk out our role and purpose here on earth.

We are to be in step and in tune with Heaven. But if we have no idea who God is or who we are, we struggle to really understand and walk in our true purpose. As we begin to see we have a high calling and a significant purpose, it becomes clear why the enemy has made such an effort to keep us in the dark regarding our true identity and the authority we carry as sons and daughters of God. As we begin to walk in our God-given identity, aware of who we are and whose we are, we will be able to accomplish our unique and God-given purposes and carry His light into the darkness, bringing forth His will and kingdom on the earth.

Nine

It's Okay to Trust Him

Trust in the One who created you.

How can I just say that? Well, I had to work through my own process, but I can now testify and say He really is for you and He truly delights in you. He is a God who can be trusted with anything.

After I came back to the faith in 2009, I struggled with learning to grow and walk in a relationship with Him. I was inconsistent in my quiet times with Him. I fell back into my old ways before college of going to church and just checking off the boxes, but deep down, there was this yearning in me for more of Him. In 2013, my husband Jason and I had our first child, a son named Toby. Toby was born on the 4th of July, and his story is definitely a testimony of who we are today. See, shortly after he was born, we noticed discoloration and a bruise to his shoulder which the doctors initially thought was just from delivery. After doing an ultrasound to confirm it wasn't a hemo meningioma, they discharged us from the hospital to go home and take care of our new bundle of joy.

Two weeks later, while rocking him to sleep after he had been super gassy that day, I noticed a huge hard bump on his right thigh. I honestly was so tired I didn't think too much about it except I couldn't figure out what the heck it was, as it was definitely not a bone. Thankfully, the next day was his two-week checkup, so I asked the doctor about it while we were there. She took a look at the bump and then stepped out to bring two other doctors in to look at it. I knew something was off. We were sent to imaging next door for x-rays and ultrasounds, and shortly afterward, we received a call that all of the scans they had done revealed nothing. The doctor then told us she had called Children's Hospital and set up an appointment with a doctor for Toby to be seen. I remember pulling up the name of the doctor to see "Oncology" next to his name, and my heart sank. I arrived home that night and put him to sleep and lay on the staircase of our townhome shouting, "Why this Lord? Why our son?" I was scared to even talk about it, but ultimately, I was angry, heartbroken, and scared of the possible scenarios ahead of us.

Looking back now, it was in those moments that I knew deep down in my spirit that the Lord was saying to me: "Lindsey, will you trust me to take care of Toby, your firstborn?" I can honestly say I had many conversations with Him, wrestling with whether or not He was really for me; whether or not I could trust Him. I was terrified of experiencing a replay of my senior year. I remember landing at this conclusion: "God, I walked away last time, and it didn't really go well. But I trust you, that you are not out to harm Toby or punish us and you care for my family." This was my heart's prayer during this season.

Toby went through many appointments, biopsies, and tests before He was even four months old. He was diagnosed with a rare tumor disorder that, although benign, was known for the rapid rate at which the tumors grow and spread. His first scan only showed five tumors, but when we rescanned him two months later, there were over seventy tumors present. It was then they started him on chemo. That in and of itself was another internal battle and conversation with the Lord. My mothering heart cried out for my son, and the Lord began showing me He was with me, and I could trust Him through it all. My relationship with Him grew as I began to sit at His feet, opening His Word and just taking it all in. That doesn't mean that it was an easy process.

There were moments of anger, frustration, fear of the unknown, and if I'm honest, numbness. I went through so many emotions and often was exhausted and spent, not just physically, but emotionally, spiritually, and mentally as well. Still, the questions I got the most were, "How are you okay?" and "How do you seem so at peace?" Of course, I know now that throughout all those long days of Toby being in and out of appointments, scans, and chemo treatments, God was there, and He was holding me close. I might have looked strong and brave, but it was Him holding me up through the hospital stays, the low white counts, the endless needles and pokes that I watched him endure as an infant, the ER visits when he would spike a temperature because he had a mediport in, or the week we were in the hospital before he turned one.

It was shortly after Toby's first birthday that he completed the rounds of chemo, and the scans showed all of the tumors had shrunk and most of them were no longer visible. Although chemo was done, we still had repeat scans for almost five years after that. I'll never forget receiving the news on July 11, 2016, that Toby's tumors were gone, and the frequent scans were done. He would still need a yearly scan for two more years, but the oncology team said the numbers and scans had stayed within normal range and Toby was healed. I still get emotional to this day as I think back to that moment. I can still feel all the joy that came with those words. My baby was healed. I still see the prayers answered each time I look at my son. The beautiful thing is that Toby's name means "God is good," which is in and of itself a testimony. It was in this season I fully began to learn that the Lord was a good God, that He could be trusted, and that He was asking me, His daughter, to trust Him even in the pain and trial.

So many of us have been let down by people we looked up to here on Earth. We have a hard time believing that someone will not let us down because we have all been disappointed and hurt at some point by people we trusted. The problem is we often project people's flaws and weaknesses onto God and start doubting that He really is for us, and He is perfect in His love for us. Trust comes from *relationship*. It comes from knowing whether a person can be taken at their word or not. When we doubt God, it is because we don't know Him well enough to know that He has fulfilled every promise He has ever made since the beginning of time. It is through time with a person that we begin to see them for who they really are. It is through intimacy with them in the rough moments, trials, and suffering that we know they will come through when they say they will. It is confidence in their character, knowing we can depend on them to be faithful and genuine in every setting and circumstance. This is what trust in our Father looks like as well: having full confidence in His character, knowing that He is who He says He is, and He will always do what He says He will do.

I think about the woman at the well found in John 4:1-42. This was a woman who'd had multiple husbands and had likely experienced a lot of hurt and disappointment in her life. She was looking for something in a relationship that she clearly wasn't finding in the men she was with. But then one day, she went to pull up water from the well. She went in the heat of the day when she thought nobody else would be there. That's when she met Jesus—a man so different from any she had met before. He spoke to her in love and compassion, and He told her things that were true about herself and her life. In the moment, she felt ashamed, uncomfortable with him being there, yet as the conversation grew, she knew that this man, Jesus, was the Truth, and she trusted He was exactly who He said He was, the Son of God. She believed so wholeheartedly that she ran and told her whole village, all those she had been avoiding, about Jesus and what He had told her.

David is another who trusted God. Time and time again, we see throughout David's story, He trusted in who God said He was. He trusted His character and His Word. From a young age, David trusted God to protect Him while tending to his father's sheep. He battled bears and lions. David spent so much time talking to God, as he tended the flock, that he grew to really *know* Him. When he went to the battleground in 1 Samuel 17:26-54, to fight Goliath, he fully trusted that the God he'd grown to know in the pastures would provide for him. He grabbed his stones and slingshot and ran, declaring in confidence, "You come to me with a sword and with a spear and with a javelin, but I come to you in the name of the Lord of hosts, the God of the armies of Israel, whom you have defied" (1 Samuel 17:45).

He knew God would defeat his enemy and trusted Him, even when it looked like his opponent was impossible to overcome. He continued to trust the Lord through years of uncertainty and life-threatening circumstances afterward. We see him repeatedly pouring his heart out to the Lord in desperation but always coming back to "I trust in you, O Lord" (Psalm 31:14). Even in his cries of "How long, O Lord?" (Psalm 13:1, 89:46), he was still trusting God to come through. He was not questioning if but when God would provide. He knew the Lord could be trusted, no matter how long it would be until his prayers were answered.

I love Proverbs 3:5-6, in The Passion Translation: "Trust in the Lord completely, and do not rely on your own opinions. With all your heart, rely on Him to guide you, and He will lead you in every decision you make. Become intimate with Him in whatever you do, and He will lead you wherever you go." The word "trust" here is the Hebrew word "batach,"[20] which means "to have confidence in, to be bold and secure in." This means to believe, without a shadow of a doubt, what God says is true, what He says is right, what He says is good, and what he has planned for you is the best way to go. The phrase "do not rely" or in the ESV translation "do not lean" is the Hebrew word "sha`an,"[21] which is an action verb meaning "to lean into God, to support oneself upon, to rest in." This means we have to take action, rest in Abba, lean close to Him, and learn His heart for us. This leads to understanding His plan for us is good, and even when our circumstances tell us otherwise, His plan for us is good and pure. The phrase "intimate with Him" in the ESV translation is "acknowledge him." It translates to the word "yada,"[22] a verb meaning "to know, learn to know, perceive and see, find out and discern and to be advised and instructed by." As I was studying and writing, looking up the meanings of these words and phrases, this is the paraphrase I felt the Lord put in my spirit: "Have confidence. Be bold and secure in the Lord with everything! Do not support yourself, but trust in God on your journey for direction. Perceive, and see; declare and discern what is right, letting Him lead you and approve of your way of living."

In these verses, we are not called to only sit and wait but to actually take action. The best part is that there's a promise. Did you notice the promise at the end? If we trust Him and lean into Him, He will lead us down the right paths. In The Passion Translation, it says we are to be "intimate with Him in whatever we do," and the ESV version states that we are to do this "in all our ways," meaning in everything we do. From the time we wake up to the time our heads hit the pillow again, we are called to trust and to lean into him.

What if we started to live this way, asking God each day, "What do you want me to do today?" Or "What do you want me to say to someone today?" It is amazing to think of what could happen if we took the time to ask God these questions. Everything would begin to have purpose-the stores we enter, the spot we park in, the words we speak to our spouse, the things we do with our kids, or the mundane errands we have that day. We would see more of the way we are supposed to live, the purpose and divine appointments He has for each of us—the interactions with people we often miss because we are so busy and distracted. What if we trusted Him enough to actually ask Him and listen?

Remember my opening testimony? The next step of Him

setting me free was teaching me to truly trust Him. I remember saying to Him: "Okay, Abba. What do I do next then? Now that the fear and darkness have silenced, what do you want me to do next?" I remember Him telling me very clearly to make another appointment so I could get a second opinion, so I made an appointment with one of the nurse practitioners. I had prayer warriors on-call praying over me and for this IUD device to either fall out or for it to be easily found so I would not have to undergo the invasive procedure they had suggested originally.

I remember going into that appointment and praying, "Lord, I know you are here with me, and whatever the circumstance, I trust you." I was not in the office for more than fifteen minutes. As my friends had been praying, it literally had almost fallen out on its own, and the NP had no problem removing it. I remember her saying, "Well, that wasn't hard. No idea why they said they couldn't find it!" I remember telling her it was because it was an answer to prayer! I left knowing that no matter how big or small our requests are, that Abba God is trustworthy and true, and I began to give thanks to Him.

I think we struggle with trusting Him because so often we don't acknowledge Him in our everyday lives or even think to ask what is on His heart for that day. I know I did. If you're struggling with trust, I would challenge you to spend a week asking Him what is on His heart and what He wants you to do each day. If you struggle with not hearing Him, I would suggest you close your eyes and write the first thing that comes to your mind or the first thing you see. Then, ask Him to confirm to you if it is from Him or not. He has a great way of confirming things with us. As I have put this into practice in my own life, I have grown in intimacy with the Father, and through intimacy, I have learned to truly trust Him. I no longer have to force myself to trust Him out of obligation or head knowledge. Now, I trust Him because I know Him.

The Lord is calling us into things that are deeper than we can perceive or understand, and often, where He asks us to step seems scary and unsafe. Going deeper with Him involves wrestling between our flesh and our spirit, knowing that although we are fearful, the Father has something better in store for us than we do for ourselves. The Lord gave me a dream several years ago that has always stuck with me. I was on the edge of a really tall cliff, and below, the water was raging and deep, and the sea was crashing onto the rocks below. I knew, in the dream, the Lord was asking me to jump and to trust Him.

I battled jumping off that cliff, but deep down in my spirit, I knew that what was in the water with Him was much better than anything that kept me lingering at the edge of this cliff, so I jumped. I began to sink to the bottom, and I remember literally feeling the sense that I was drowning. As I began to sink under the water and lose oxygen, I saw a figure who I knew was Jesus, and He began to breathe life into my mouth underneath the water. As He did so, my body began to be revived, and He said, "Follow me." As I began to swim in the depths of the water, He took me to a place in the middle of the ocean that I'll never forget. In the middle of the dark and raging ocean, a village with a majestic palace came into view. As I got closer, the water seemed to disappear, the land came beneath my feet, and I began to walk, following the One who had breathed life into my mouth.

Many of us are standing on the edge of the cliff, lingering. We are scared of jumping because we fear the unknown. So many "what-if's" fill our minds as we contemplate whether or not we will go where He is calling. Yet, it is when we actually do jump, He takes us deeper. It often feels like we made the wrong move and we are drowning, but then He comes close and breathes life into us. He takes us to a place we never knew was hidden there under the deep waters, a place that is majestic and peaceful, where our feet find dry ground. This process is one of killing the flesh and cutting off the things that hold us back from what He is calling us to. It requires a surrender that often looks and feels terrifying, but He is with us and has our good in mind. He is our true security and trusting Him is always our best bet.

Ten

Give Him Praise for the Promises

*Keep trusting in the Lord and do what is right in
His eyes. Fix your heart on the promises of God and
you will be secure, feasting on his faithfulness.*

Psalm 37:3, TPT

*Let the word of Christ live in you richly, flooding you
with all wisdom. Apply the Scriptures as you teach and
instruct one another with the Psalms, and with festive
praises, and with prophetic songs given to you
spontaneously by the Spirit, so sing to God with all
your hearts! Let every activity of your lives and every
word that comes from your lips be drenched with
the beauty of our Lord Jesus, the Anointed One. And
bring your constant praise to God the Father because
of what Christ has done for you!*

Colossians 3:16-17, TPT

This is the best part—the part where we take all the Father has
spoken and begin to praise Him for it, even if it hasn't come
to pass yet. This is what we stand on, this is what we wage
war with, and this is what keeps us planted firmly as we climb
higher up the mountain to Him. You see, it's our praise, honor,

and worship that brings glory to Him, the One who created and rules over everything. He has known from the beginning of time what the end of time will hold. That is just mind-blowing to me. He promises He will have victory over the kingdom of darkness. He promises we will make our home with Him forever if we call upon His name and by faith acknowledge our need for Him and the blood His Son shed for us.

Praising the King brings us closer to Him—closer to His heart. Heaven's heart is ushered in when we fall down and worship, singing praises to Him for what He has done, what He is doing, and what He will do. Just like in any relationship, affections are stirred when love is expressed. God's affections for us are stirred when we pour out praise to Him, and his response is an outpouring of love on us (which then in turn stirs our affections for him even more).

Throughout the Word, we see the angels in Heaven worshiping the King who is seated on the throne. In Revelation, the elders lay their crowns down at his feet and worship Him. You see, the promises He speaks to us aren't just meant for our time on earth, but they continue to be fulfilled in Heaven. Jesus tells us in Matthew 6:19-21, that treasures are being stored up in Heaven for us and as we faithfully serve Him here, we will see the fulfillment of and the reward for the things we have sown. That is the beauty of serving an infinite King. His Word continues for eternity.

Praising Him for His promises can simply be worshiping Him with the words He has spoken to us. It's a conversation we start with Him, sometimes just beginning with giving thanks for the things around us, which then turns into a beautiful conversation of prayer and praise between us and our King. Start with reading the sample prayer below and then let it continue with your own words.

"Lord, I know that what you say is true. I know that you have never lied and that your word cannot return void. I stand on your promises, declaring yes and amen to the words you have spoken over me. I know that I may not yet have seen them come to pass, but I know that your voice is true. I know that you are the Creator of everything. I know that we are your sons and daughters, created with an ultimate purpose, to glorify you. I know that you have spoken promises since the beginning of time, and you have kept every one of them. You have the ultimate track record, so Abba, I'm trusting that even though I don't understand and can't see it, you are good for your Word. Your mercy extends from the throne to those you call your children. You are abounding in steadfast love. You are just. You are gracious. You are good. You are the Beginning and the End. You have overcome, and you rewrote history to come and redeem us. You are worthy. You are holy, holy, holy. You are never-ending. Your presence never leaves us. You are the faithful One who wants the best for His children. You are victorious. You are mighty. Your strength and hand chase out our enemies, and your strength knows no end. You take our yokes and give us rest within your arms. To your throne be exaltation and glory! May we your people see you and rejoice! I stand on these truths and promises and give thanks for them saying yes and amen!"

The psalmist was great at writing songs of praise. I love Psalm 86, where we read the words of a son desperately crying out to his Father to hear his pleas for help. He asks his Father to lean down, listen, and see the evil he is enduring. Then, he begins to speak the promises of the Lord, to recall who God is, what He has done, and what He has said He will do. The posture changes in his heart. That praise and worship and remembering all that the Father has said and done is key in changing our mindsets when we are anxious or troubled.

The promises of God are found throughout the whole Bible. We can turn to practically any page and find a promise spoken by Him. Even on the very first pages, we see a promise given to Adam and Eve—that a seed of woman would come and crush the enemy's head (Genesis 3:15). God's promise in the garden was fulfilled in the birth of Jesus and forever changed the way we as believers get to approach Him and sit in His presence. How amazing is it that God loves us enough that He has had a plan since the beginning to save His children? He is that good and that amazing! Thank you, Father, for the promise of Your Son. Since the beginning, in the garden, you had a redemption story written.

We read in Genesis, just a few chapters after the first promise, God spoke to Noah and told him a flood was coming. He asked Noah to trust Him and build an ark in order to save his family and every species of animal. Well, the ark wasn't built overnight. It would have taken Noah years to build, gathering lumber and the supplies needed, hammering each plank together, sealing the wood with tar, etc. It would have been tedious and hard work, yet He was faithful and continued with the work God had given him to do (Genesis 6:9-22). He trusted what the Lord had spoken, and his faith was counted to Him as righteousness (Hebrews 11:7). Day in and day out, he worked to build an ark that would save his family from a flood, even though it had never even rained before. He knew if the Lord had said it, it would be. I imagine he would have become discouraged at times, but he never gave up. He would have most likely endured mockery from people around him, as it had never rained on the earth up to that point. I strongly believe his act of diligence, measuring, cutting wood, and hammering pegs were his acts of worship and praise towards God.

David, the king of Israel, was anointed to be the next king in 1 Samuel 16:12-13. The only problem was that Saul was still the king of Israel. David waited twelve to fifteen years before he became king of Israel. Not only did he have to wait on his promise, but while he was waiting, he became a servant to Saul, playing music to soothe him when he was under the attack of a tormenting spirit (1 Samuel 16:14-23). As David's journey to the throne continued, we see that he went from being victorious in battles for Saul to having to flee from the jealous king and hide from him for about seven years. He was constantly on the move and on the run from Saul, who was trying to kill him. But David had been given a promise from the Lord: "You will be my anointed one." He held onto the promise and honored Saul, even while he ran from him. Even in one of David's most vulnerable moments, when he had the chance to kill Saul, he showed him honor, trusting in God's timing for His promise to be fulfilled.

We see David often became discouraged in the journey, writing of his anguish in the poetic songs we know as the Psalms. It is believed that several of these were written while David was on the run from Saul. While in the midst of escaping and hiding from the man who tried to take his life, he wrote beautiful words of worship to God. In the Psalms David wrote, we often see his spirit is down and discouraged, disappointed at God's timing. He wavers. It is important to see that even in the midst of wavering, he begins to declare the truth and promises of who he knew God to be. One of the Psalms believed to have been written by David while on the run from Saul is Psalm 7:1-17:

O Lord my God, in you do I take refuge; save me from all my pursuers and deliver me, lest like a lion they tear my soul apart, rending it in pieces, with none to deliver. O Lord my God, if I have done this, if there is wrong in my hands, if I have repaid my friend with evil or plundered my enemy without cause, let the enemy pursue my soul and overtake it, and let him trample my life to the ground and lay my glory in the dust. Arise, O Lord, in your anger; lift yourself up against the fury of my enemies; awake for me; you have appointed a judgment. Let the assembly of the peoples be gathered about you; over it return on high. The Lord judges the peoples; judge me, O Lord, according to my righteousness and according to the integrity that is in me. Oh, let the evil of the wicked come to an end, and may you establish the righteous— you who test the minds and hearts, O righteous God! My shield is with God, who saves the upright in heart. God is a righteous judge, and a God who feels indignation every day. If a man does not repent, God will whet His sword; He has bent and readied His bow; He has prepared for him his deadly weapons, making his arrows fiery shafts. Behold, the wicked man conceives evil and is pregnant with mischief and gives birth to lies. He makes a pit, digging it out, and falls into the

Give Him Praise for the Promises

hole that he has made. His mischief returns upon his own head, and on his own skull his violence descends. I will give to the Lord the thanks due to His righteousness, and I will sing praise to the name of the Lord, the Most High.

Psalm 7

David questions whether he brought all this on himself. He seems discouraged in verses 3-5, yet he declares the truth that God is the One who judges the people. He writes and sings the truth—that God is his shield and the One "who saves the upright in heart" (vs 10). He acknowledges God as a just and righteous judge, and he gives thanks for it. David begins singing praises to the One who created Him.

Praise and worship to God can also be as songs of praise for who He is!

Praise the Lord, all nations! Extol him, all people! For great is His steadfast love toward us, and the faithfulness of the Lord endures forever! Praise the Lord!

Psalm 117

Praise the Lord! Yes, give praise, O servants of the Lord. Praise the name of the Lord! Blessed be the name of the Lord now and forever. Everywhere—from east to west—praise the name of the Lord. For the Lord is high above the nations; his glory is higher than the heavens. Who can be compared with the Lord our God, who is enthroned on high? He stoops to look down on Heaven and on earth. He lifts the poor from the dust and the needy from the garbage dump. He

*sets them among princes, even the princes of his
own people! He gives the childless woman a
family, making her a happy mother. Praise the Lord!*

Psalm 113

There is something that shifts in us as we worship and praise the Lord. When we humble ourselves before Him and lie at His feet, declaring and singing back to Him all His glory, majesty, and goodness, the atmosphere around us shifts. I have seen it in my own home so many times. When everyone seems to be having a bad day, I will often turn on worship music and start to dance and sing with the kids, and sometimes hubby even joins in when he's not working. Our spirits are lifted, and we shift from complaining and moping to remembering the truth about our God. We are filled with joy! Some days the worship music just stays on all day long, helping us take captive our thoughts and renewing our mindsets to the worship and praise of the Lion of Judah who is seated on the right hand of the throne of God. It helps us to remember His blood that was shed for us. It conquers the thoughts we struggle with and the flesh we give into and sets our minds back on Him.

Promises of God

God still speaks promises over us today. We know there are still many unfulfilled promises in Scripture for us as God's children, but He also speaks specific promises to us individually. We often assume the "Word of God" is strictly in reference to Scripture. However, two different Greek words for "word" are used in the Bible: "logos" and "rhema." "Logos" refers to the written Word of God—the Bible, while "rhema," means "an utterance or spoken word." Rhema is the still small voice we sense in our spirits as the Holy Spirit speaks to us. It can also come in the form of prophetic words given by the Holy Spirit, spoken through the mouths of His people. In the context of promises, I believe it is important to see that rhema words are words spoken but also tested against the logos Word of God. In 1 Thessalonians 5:20, we are told, "Do not despise the prophecies, but test everything; hold fast to what is good." We see this lived out in Acts 17:11 as the Bereans received the rhema word of God through Paul and Silas. They checked the Scriptures to see if what they had been told was the truth.

Many of us have experienced receiving a promise from God, but after some time goes by, it seems like it will never come to pass. Or maybe we have heard Him tell us of a certain gift He has given us or purpose He has called us to, but when it doesn't happen when we want, we accuse the Lord of having forgotten or we start doubting the word He gave us. I have been discouraged when thinking the Lord was clearly speaking to me, but the fulfillment of what He said felt impossible or just so far away from actually happening. Instead of staying in this state of discouragement or doubt, I have to remember to shift my mindset back to what I know to be true. There are countless examples in the Bible where God made a promise to His children that took many years to be fulfilled.

What are some of the promises of God? I often feel that when we need to praise and declare these, we can't remember because our minds are spiraling. I want this to be a section where, even after you read this book, you will pick it up, turn to it, and use it again as a weapon of praise! Our voices of praise are mighty in the spirit realm. Singing in our spirits, dancing around to music, or declaring praise out loud are all things we can use to shift our hearts and minds and refocus them back on the One who is worthy, rather than on the natural circumstances around us.

I encourage you to start studying the promises of God. There are hundreds of them in Scripture, and the best part is that we too get to cling on to those promises and claim them for ourselves. The Bible wasn't just written some thousands of years ago to tell a historical story—nope! Every page is God-breathed. The Bible says, "For we have the living Word of God, which is full of energy, like a two-mouthed sword. It will even penetrate to the very core of our being where soul and spirit, bone and marrow meet! It interprets and reveals the true thoughts and secret motives of our hearts" (Hebrews 4:12, TPT). This means the words found within the Bible are alive, they are active, and they still penetrate the hearts of man. It means what He said to Adam, Abraham, Moses, David, the prophets, the disciples, Paul, and many others, is just as true today as it was then.

His words haven't changed, and His promises haven't changed, so use them and claim them for yourself. Take them and bind them to your heart, putting them before your eyes and in your homes, just like Deuteronomy 6, says. Teach them to your family, and study them. He is faithful to fulfill His promises, and all His Words are true, so worship and praise the Lord. Praise Him for His promises, and shout them out loud in the midst of the battles you fight. Speak, and declare them in your homes and over your children and families. Sing praises, and make songs with the Scriptures the Lord has placed on your heart, for He is great and His love for us never fails. Father, we say *yes* and *amen* to your promises! We praise you for your promises!

One of my favorite verses that has to do with the promises of God says: "For all the promises of God find their Yes in him. That is why it is through him that we utter our Amen to God for his glory" (2 Corinthians 1:20). The word "yes" here is the Greek word *"nai,"* which means "a strong affirmation to something, often used as verily, verily."[23] When we utter "yes and amen," we are agreeing with what the Father has done, what He is doing, and what He will do! We are coming into agreement with heaven!

I pray that as we begin to understand these truths, they take root in our minds, bodies, and spirits. In the appendix, I have listed just some of the Promises of God and verses I like to declare out loud. I have been known to put them in song and sing them over myself, my children, or my home. I use them to wage war in the spirit when I feel the enemy creeping into my mind, whispering lies about who God is or who I am. I pray as you read these, you will grab hold of them and declare His promises out loud! Make your own songs, worship, and art. Let your creativity flow from how His Spirit speaks to and moves you.

Conclusion: Your Crown Awaits

So...here's your call to action!

Do you remember that sticky note I told you to grab at the beginning of this book? I want you to look back at it. What have you learned since initially writing down who you are and what would you like to add today as you finish the last pages of this book?

My prayer is that you have begun to see who you are in light of who God is. That is the intent of this whole book, to point you to the truth of who you are in Christ Jesus. The adventure has just begun. When we begin to walk in the light of who we were created to be, we begin to walk boldly as carriers of light into this dark world. As Isaiah says:

"Arise, shine, for your light has come, and the glory of the Lord has risen upon you. For behold, darkness shall cover the earth, and thick darkness the peoples; but the Lord will arise upon you, and his glory will be seen upon you."

Isaiah 61:1-3

We, as sons and daughters of God, are the ones who radiate His glory to the earth. We are the ones called to walk into the darkness and light it up. We can do this because the Light of the world is in us. We are told the days will get darker and that thick darkness will cover the people, for they will be blinded by the darkness, but what seems to be hopeless carries much hope. In that one conjunction we see: BUT the Lord will arise upon us, and His glory will be seen in us.

Many of us will be called into areas of darkness that seem scary, but as we begin to walk in authority, true daughters and sons, our light will begin to shine hope around us, radiating as a bright beacon. It is time for us to let our "light shine before all men so that they may see your good works and glorify our Father who is in Heaven" (Matthew 5:16, NKJV). The calling today is the same as the day those words were written; the kingdom is the same as it has always been. It is time for us to walk in this understanding and carry the message of Jesus, the King of Hope, Love, and Peace into our circles of influence.

Are you ready to walk in your true identity?

Appendix

Prayers of Declaring God's Promises

God is Faithful

"Know therefore that the Lord your God is God, the faithful God who keeps covenant and steadfast love with those who love Him and keep His commandments, to a thousand generations..."
Deuteronomy 7:9

You, God, are the faithful One. You have kept every promise that has been uttered out of Your mouth, and You will keep every one of Your promises! For Your love is steadfast, never-ending, and it continues on as far as the east is from the west, never turning away from Your children. Generation after generation, You have been faithful, and You will be forever!

God Protects

We know that everyone who has been born of God does not keep on sinning, but he who was born of God protects him, and the

evil one does not touch him.
1 John 5:18

"Because he holds fast to me in love, I will deliver
him; I will protect him, because he knows my name.
When he calls to me, I will answer him; I will be with
him in trouble; I will rescue him and honor him."
Psalm 91:14-15

Your Word, oh Lord, says You protect those who seek refuge and shelter in You. The Psalms tell us that You cover in the shelter of Your arms those who hold fast to You, never letting them go. You cover them and hide them from the evil one. For You are the true God, strong and mighty, Yahweh, the Great I AM. So, I hold fast to Your truth that You are the Protector, and I declare protection over (fill in the blank).

Nothing is Too Hard for God

"Behold, I am the Lord, the God of all flesh.
Is anything too hard for me?"
Jeremiah 32:27

Jesus looked at them and said, "With man it is
impossible, but not with God. For all things
are possible with God."
Mark 10:27

But he said, "What is impossible with
man is possible with God."
Luke 18:27

For although the way seems impossible, oh Lord, while walking in Your steps, nothing is impossible. I trust that what You have spoken in the quiet places and in Your Word will not fail. For Your Word never returns void! So I stand on Your Word that says what seems impossible with man is never impossible with You. Give me eyes to see what You see. Give me ears to hear what You are speaking. Holy Spirit, lead my steps.

The One Who Fears the Lord Will Lack Nothing

Oh, taste and see that the Lord is good! Blessed is the man who takes refuge in Him! Oh, fear the Lord, you His saints, for those who fear Him have no lack! The young lions suffer want and hunger; but those who seek the Lord lack no good thing.
Psalm 34:8-10

Lord, give me Your eyes to see. Awaken my senses to know You are good! For You are God. You are the Creator of all things. You hold everything together. So, when You say "go," things will go. When You speak, things come to life. Every need I have, You already know. Give me a heart of trust; set my eyes on You, knowing that Your timing is perfect, and You will provide for my every need. Your Word says I will lack nothing, for everything is complete in You. In Jesus' name, amen!

Blessed Are Those Who Trust God

"Blessed is the man who trusts in the Lord, whose trust is the Lord. He is like a tree planted by water,

that sends out its roots by the stream, and does not
fear when heat comes, for its leaves remain green,
and is not anxious in the year of drought, for it
does not cease to bear fruit."
Jeremiah 17:7-8

Blessed are the ones who trust in the Lord and who make the Lord their resting place. Lord, let me be one who trusts in You like the tree planted by the water, knowing that even when the heat comes, my leaves will remain green, for my trust is in You, and I know You are there. When it does not seem like things are coming to fruition, I trust Your timing is always perfect, and You will be the One who pours life into me until that time. In Jesus' name. Amen.

God is Always With Us

"Have I not commanded you? Be strong and courageous.
Do not be frightened, and do not be dismayed, for
the Lord your God is with you wherever you go."
Joshua 1:9

Lord, I know You are always with me, just like You were with Joshua, and just like You were with Your people. They had no need to fear or be worried because You were with them no matter where they went. I declare You are with me today and that no spirit of fear can come near me, in Jesus' name. For I am Your child, and You make me strong and courageous!

He Restores What is Broken

He restores my soul. He leads me in paths
of righteousness for His name's sake.
Psalm 23:3

And after you have suffered a little while, the God
of all grace, who has called you to His eternal
glory in Christ, will Himself restore, confirm,
strengthen, and establish you.
1 Peter 5:10

Abba, in the pain of what feels broken, You are there. You don't leave us broken; instead, your Word says You restore us. Even though we suffer, You will restore and strengthen us. When my soul feels like it is breaking into pieces, You pick it up and put it back together. For in the midst of what feels painful, You are gently restoring me into something more. For You are the Potter, and I am the clay. Mold me and make me like You, putting every piece back in a way that reflects Your masterful hand.

He is Our Refuge

The Lord is the strength of His people; He is the
saving refuge of His anointed.
Psalm 28:8

...for you have been my refuge, a strong
tower against the enemy.
Psalm 61:3

The name of the Lord is a strong tower;
the righteous man runs into it and is safe.
Proverbs 18:10

In the nights when the darkness seems to creep in, in the moments when it feels like all is lost, when the world seems to have fallen apart, when chaos and confusion come, I have nothing to fear or worry about because You are my refuge. You are my safe dwelling place. In You alone do I find rest, and in You I receive strength. For You cover me in your arms, holding me and covering me in Your mighty wings. To You be the glory, for You are a refuge and strong tower for Your children!

He Binds Up the Brokenhearted

The Spirit of the Lord God is upon me, because the
Lord has anointed me to bring good news to the poor;
He has sent me to bind up the brokenhearted, to
proclaim liberty to the captives, and the opening
of the prison to those who are bound...
Isaiah 61:1

He heals the brokenhearted and binds up their wounds.
Psalm 147:3

Yahweh! Great are You, oh God, worthy of all praise and adoration. You bind up the broken, You set captives free, and You open up the prison doors of those who have been bound. You see every wound we have, and You call it out so You can step in to redeem and restore it. Take my wounds, and bind them up. I trust You are faithful, and I trust Your heart is for me

to be set free. Where the Spirit of the Lord is, there is freedom!
In Jesus' name.

He is Our Hope

*So it is impossible for God to lie, for we know
that His promise and His vow will never change!
And now we have run into His heart to hide ourselves
in His faithfulness. This is where we find His strength
and comfort, for He empowers us to seize what has
already been established ahead of time—an
unshakeable hope! We have this certain hope like a
strong, unbreakable anchor holding our souls to
God Himself. Our anchor of hope is fastened to
the mercy seat which sits in the heavenly realm
beyond the sacred threshold, and where Jesus,
our forerunner, has gone in before us. He is now
and forever our royal Priest like Melchizedek.*
Hebrews 6:18-20, TPT

King Jesus, You alone are the royal Priest. You took on all
our sins—past, present, and future. You stepped in to be the
ultimate sacrifice and poured out Your blood on the mercy
seat in the throne room of Heaven. You deserve all praises
and glory and honor. I declare that my hope is in You and You
alone. For it is because of You that I can run and hide in Your
faithful arms. You promise You will never change, so I can rest
knowing that all my hope is in You—the unchangeable one!

He Sets Us Free

"So if the Son sets you free, you will be free indeed."
John 8:36

For the law of the Spirit of life has set you free
in Christ Jesus from the law of sin and death.
Romans 8:2

Now the Lord is the Spirit, and where the
Spirit of the Lord is, there is freedom.
2 Corinthians 3:17

I am free! I am free! I am a daughter set free because of the blood of the Lamb. For Your Word says that in Jesus and through His blood, I have been set free. You have set me free from condemnation, free from being a slave to the law, free from the reign of sin, and free from the dominion of the evil one. For in You is freedom! I declare I want to walk in Your freedom. Holy Spirit, I invite You in to show me the areas where I am still struggling. Your Word, oh Lord, promises that in You I am set free! Break off the chains that hold me captive. Break off the mindsets that I am stuck in. Pour Your Spirit out on me so I can see what You see, hear what You hear, and think with a kingdom mindset through Your Spirit within me! To You be all the glory! In Jesus' name.

Notes

1. Simmons, Brian, and Candace Simmons. 2015. The Sacred Journey: God's Relentless Pursuit of Our Affection. Racine, WI: Broadsheet Publishing.

2. "H4686 - Matsuwd - Strong's Hebrew Lexicon (ESV)." Blue Letter Bible. Accessed June 17, 2020. https://www.blueletterbible.org/lang/lexicon/lexicon.cfm?Strongs=H4686&t=ESV

3. "Redeem." Merriam-Webster. Accessed April 27, 2021. https://www.merriam-webster.com/dictionary/redeem.

4. "G3140 - Martyreō - Strong's Greek Lexicon (ESV)." Blue Letter Bible. Accessed September 15, 2020. https://www.blueletterbible.org/lang/lexicon/lexicon.cfm?Strongs=G3140&t=eSV.

5. YouTube. August 06, 2020. Accessed September 10, 2020. https://youtu.be/fp62p7EvzaI.

6. "G25 - Agapaō - Strong's Greek Lexicon (ESV)." Blue Letter Bible. Accessed July 23, 2020. https://www.blueletterbible.org/lang/lexicon/lexicon.cfm?Strongs=G25&t=ESV.

7. "G5590 - Psychē - Strong's Greek Lexicon (ESV)." Blue Letter Bible. Accessed September 09, 2020. https://www.blueletterbible.org/lang/lexicon/lexicon.cfm?Strongs=G5590&t=ESV.

8. "G4151 - Pneuma - Strong's Greek Lexicon (ESV)." Blue Letter Bible. Accessed September 09, 2020. https://www.blueletterbible.org/lang/lexicon/lexicon. cfm?Strongs=G4151&t=ESV.

9. https://www.merriam-webster.com/dictionary/religion

10. Simmons, Brian, and Candace Simmons. 2015. The Sacred Journey: God's Relentless Pursuit of Our Affection. Racine, WI: Broadsheet Publishing.

11. Google Search. Accessed February 13, 2021. https://www.google.com/search?q=google dictionary online&rlz=1CAWAFN_enUS777US778&oq=google dictionary&aqs=chrome.5.69i57j0i433l2j0l2j0i433j0 i13l1i433j0l3.7113j0j7&sourceid=chrome&ie=UTF-8#dobs=communion.

12. "Intimate Relationship." Wikipedia. March 04, 2021. Accessed January 05, 2021. https://en.wikipedia.org/wiki/Intimate_relationship.

13. Bockarova, Mariana. Ph.D. Accessed November 15, 2020. https://www.psychologytoday.com/us/blog/romantically-attached/201802/the-7-elements-define-intimate-relationship

14. "G3340 - Metanoeō - Strong's Greek Lexicon (ESV)." Blue Letter Bible. Accessed January 09, 2021. https://www.blueletterbible.org/lang/lexicon/lexicon. cfm?Strongs=G3340&t=ESV

15. G365 - Ananeoō - Stong's Greek Lexicon (ESV). Blue Letter Bible. Accessed June 23, 2021. https://www.blueletterbible.org/lexicon/g365/esv/mgnt/0-1/.

16. Leaf, Caroline. Switch on Your Brain: The Key to Peak Happiness, Thinking, and Health. Grand Rapids, MI: BakerBooks, a Division of Baker Publishing Group, 2015.

17. Naus, Rev. Eric. "God's Feminine Attributes." The Moody Church. Accessed September 22, 2020. https://www.moodychurch.org/gods-feminine-attributes/

18. Naus, Rev. Eric. "God's Feminine Attributes." The Moody Church. Accessed September 22, 2020. https://www.moodychurch.org/gods-feminine-attributes/

19. Vallotton, Kris. Fashioned to Reign: Empowering Women to Fulfill Their Divine Destiny. Minneapolis, MN: Chosen, a Division of Baker Publishing Group, 2014.

20. H982 - bātah - Strong's Hebrew Lexicon (ESV). Accessed June 23, 2021. https://www.blueletterbible.org/lexicon/h982/esv/wlc/0-1/.

21. H8172 - šāʾan - Strong's Hebrew Lexicon (ESV). Accessed June 23, 2021. https://www.blueletterbible.org/lexicon/h8172/esv/wlc/0-1/.

22. H3045 - yādaʾ - Strong's Hebrew Lexicon (ESV). Accessed June 23, 2021.https://www.blueletterbible.org/lexicon/h8172/esv/wlc/0-1/.

23. "G3483 - Nai - Strong's Greek Lexicon (ESV)." Blue Letter Bible. Accessed Jan. & Feb., 2021. https://www.blueletterbible.org/lang/lexicon/lexicon.cfm?Strongs=G3483&t=ESV.

About the Author

Lindsey Renee is an author, faith teacher, wife, and mother. She wrote the book 45 Days of Prayer, A Prayer Journal & Guide, and is the co-host of the Arrow Women podcast. As a ministry leader, Lindsey is devoted to seeing women grow in their gifts and power as they come into the Throne Room. Her heart and passion is for every woman to know how loved they are by the Father, and to walk in their true identities as daughters of the Most High King. Lindsey is based in the Washington D.C. area with her husband Jason, three boys, and baby girl.